IS GENESIS MYTH?

The Shocking Story of the Teaching of Evolution

at

ABILENE CHRISTIAN UNIVERSITY

by

Bert Thompson, Ph.D.

(With an "Introduction" by Wayne Jackson)

APOLOGETICS PRESS, INC.
230 Landmark Drive
Montgomery, Alabama 36117-2752
Copyright 1986
ISBN: 0-932859-07-0

DEDICATION

This volume is gratefully dedicated to the courageous men and women who love truth more than life itself. These are strong souls who are not intimidated by compromising power structures. Generations yet unborn will rise up and call them "blessed."

Cover design: Wayne Jackson
Cover artwork: Mrs. Ray (Bonnie) Cobb
First printing — January, 1986 (10,000 copies)
Second printing — February, 1986 (10,000 copies)

Table of Contents

(—continued—)

Table of Contents (continued)

Introduction

Wayne Jackson
Co-Editor, *Reason & Revelation*

The Subversion Of Our Youth—A Betrayed Confidence

Several millennia ago a psalmist penned these words: "Lo, children are a heritage of Jehovah; and the fruit of the womb is his reward" (Psalm 127:3). Responsible Christian people, who have been blessed by the Lord with children, are keenly aware of the value of these precious offspring. Together with that profound sense of thanksgiving is also the sober knowledge that it is our weighty responsibility to train our youngsters in the service of the Creator, for, apart from serving the Living God, there is no real meaning to life (Ecclesiastes 12:13; Isaiah 43:7).

Rearing children to live for Jehovah is not an easy task in this wicked twentieth century. We thus seek assistance in this noble assignment from a variety of sources, one of which is the utilization of Christian colleges. Administration officials associated with our schools have promised us that if we will entrust to them our children, they will provide them with a balanced education within the framework of biblical soundness. They have pledged that while our youngsters are being prepared to enter the secular world, within the community of the Christian college their faith is being wonderfully enriched. And we believed them!

What you are about to read in the following pages of this book is a story so bizarre, so shocking, that you will initially find it incredible. No one likes to think that he has been betrayed! And yet, the evidence is so overwhelming, the documentation is so clear, that no honest investigator will be able to deny it. It is the story of the teaching of evolution—raw evolution; not presented as mere theory, but as "scientific fact," with some of the most rabidly atheistic textbooks in print used as the media of communication. The crime is not being perpetrated on the campus of some humanistically oriented institution, but from the sanctified halls of a reputedly Christian school—ABILENE CHRISTIAN UNIVERSITY.

Abilene Christian College (now a university) was founded in September of 1906 by A.B. Barret, a gospel preacher from Tennessee "who envisioned a center of Christian education in the Southwest." For almost four score years the institution has been closely associated with the churches of Christ. The "Charter" of the school states that the facility was created for the purpose of providing an education "in which the arts, sciences, languages and Holy Scriptures shall be taught, together with such other courses of instruction as shall be deemed advisable. . ." Remember that reference to the "Holy Scriptures" when you later see, in a professor's own handwriting, an allusion to the Genesis "myth"! In another document entitled, "The Purpose of Abilene Christian College" (*Staff Handbook*, 1971-1972, p 15), it is claimed that one of the functions of that institution is to **exalt the Bible as the Word of God**. That, admittedly, is a noble goal.

It is, however, the indictment of **this** book that that purpose, in flagrant violation of the aims of the founders, has been prostituted—at least by some professors at Abilene Christian University. Moreover, the publishers of this book contend that this subversion of our children's faith is not simply a recent occurrence; we have, in fact, documented proof that evolutionary errors have been propagated "on the hill" [as the university locale in Abilene is familiarly known] for **more than a decade**, and that complaints relative to the same have been ignored, denied, and concealed. Furthermore, this amazing cover-up continues to be perpetuated unto this very hour! And surely our grief about this sordid affair reached its zenith when we discovered that the Dean of the College of Biblical Studies has become a participant in the scandalous concealment!

Apparently, the "powers that be" in Abilene are secure

in the conviction that: (a) No one will believe the charges that have been made. (b) They are not accountable to the people of the churches of Christ. In fact, in their pride, certain officials have stated that they do not intend to "bend" to outside pressures—apparently no matter how "rotten" the doctrine may be [and I borrow that descriptive term from one of ACU's professors, who characterized the teaching in precisely that way]. (c) Administrators obviously feel that they are powerful enough to weather any storm that comes; the controversy will subside eventually. They may underestimate our people!

The events, of which you are about to read, commenced (from our vantage point) almost one year ago when Dr. Bert Thompson, Co-Editor of *Reason & Revelation* and Co-Director of Apologetics Press, Inc., received a letter from a very concerned biology major at Abilene Christian University. The student claimed that in some of his science courses at ACU the theory of evolution was being taught blatantly. It was not being presented as "theory," but as a factual system of belief that cannot be scientifically refuted. Moreover (and this is tremendously important to remember) it was not being taught within the context of a dialogue for scientific rebuttal; rather it was being presented as the only viable explanation of the history of earth's creatures!

Frankly, when Dr. Thompson shared this initial information with me, we both confessed that it seemed almost unbelievable. Brother Thompson, a 1971 biology graduate of ACU, did not want to believe that such could be true of his alma mater. He determined, therefore, to check out the matter thoroughly and so be convinced only on the basis of hardcore, irrefutable evidence.

The **very first thing** that Bert Thompson did was to write **personal** letters to the professors whose names had been mentioned—Drs. Kenneth Williams and Archie Manis. When that brotherly procedure secured absolutely zero results, the inquiry was intensified. As the investigation progressed across the months, materials began to come to light that left us absolutely numb. The "shenanigans" that have been perpetrated by some of those associated with ACU in regard to this matter would rival a television soap-opera.

You surely must think that I am over-stating the case. I do not blame you. However, I invite you to carefully study the material in this book. And as you read, I want you to think of the youngsters—sons and daughters like your own perhaps—who are now studying under such instructors, and being guided by such administrators, as are revealed in this narrative. You just may wish to let them know how you feel!

Stockton, California
January 1, 1986

Author's Preface

Some memories of the past never grow dim, because they are so sweet and so precious, and so deeply imbedded in the shadows of our mind. The poet put it in these words:

"Into my heart's treasury I slipped a coin,
That time cannot take, nor thief purloin;
Oh better than the minting of a gold-crowned king,
Is the safe-kept memory of a lovely thing."

One such "safe-kept memory of a lovely thing" has often filled my thoughts and my heart. I remember it just as if it was yesterday. I was a young high school graduate, fresh from the halls of Dalhart (Texas) High School. I had looked forward to this day for so long. Now it was reality! The long drive from Dalhart to Abilene had ended. My Dad, Dr. C.A. Thompson, had parked the beige pickup truck in front of Edwards Dormitory on the campus of Abilene Christian College (as it was then known). We walked into the dormitory and to the receptionist's desk. I can still remember the very first person I met on campus. His name was Jimmy, and he was so very friendly. It was like he had known me all my life. He seemed so glad to see me. He gave me my room key (I still remember the room—number 132) and my Dad and I walked down the dormitory hall to that room. I can still picture, in my mind's eye, those green walls, the metal desks, and the tile floors. And I can remember unloading every single box of clothes, books, laundry detergent, towels, and all the other paraphernalia high school graduates take to college—everything from graduation gifts to "necessities" neatly tucked into the boxes by a loving Mother who is sending her son away to college for the first time. I still remember the tears in my Mother's eyes as she sat in the truck, and the big bear-hug my Dad gave me before he got into the driver's seat that last time. I was at college, finally! But not just **any** college. I was at **Abilene Christian College**. And I was **so proud**!

There are many other memories of those wonderful four years. There are memories of roommates, memories of tests (oh, such memories), memories of professors, memories of special activities, and memories of life-long friendships which endure even to this very day. And, of course, there is the memory of that 14th day of May, 1971 when I walked across that long stage in Moody Coliseum and picked up that purple enshrouded diploma. I honestly don't know who was happier— my parents, or me. But one thing I **do** know: we both were glad "we" had succeeded. And we were so happy to be a part of the great Abilene Christian College family!

Those four years molded and formed me in more ways than I shall ever know. The things I learned while completing my B.S. degree in biology at what is now Abilene Christian University have served me well—through my graduate training at Texas A&M University, through my teaching at Texas A&M in the College of Veterinary Medicine, through my work in Christian apologetics, and even to this day through my teaching responsibilities as a Professor at the Alabama Christian School of Religion. Hanging on the wall in my office is, to this very day, that diploma—which symbolizes an institution I have loved, and still love, very deeply.

It is that love, and those memories, that make this present task so very difficult and painful. I have always been committed to my alma mater, and to Christian education in general. In fact, I left the secular university community in order to more fully commit myself to Christian education. I believe in the goals and ideals of "our" schools.

But I do **not** believe in teaching **our** children organic and/or theistic evolution as factual! And I do **not** believe in teaching that Genesis 1-2 is a myth! And I will **not** sit idly by and allow that to happen—whether at my beloved alma mater or at someone else's!

The narrative you are about to read is the sad story of one such occurrence. One year ago, as this record will reveal, I was contacted by students at Abilene Christian University—

students not only from my alma mater, but from the biology department of which I am a graduate. The story they told was nothing short of incredible! They were being taught that evolution was factual. They were being taught that Genesis 1-2 was a "myth." They were being taught that belief in organic evolution was a part of the intellectual equipment of all rational, thinking persons.

I admit that at first I was totally unprepared to accept such accusations as factual and true. I was, to be quite honest, incredulous. How could such things be happening on the campus of **my** alma mater, and in the department of which I was a graduate?! It just could not be true!

But it **is** true. And this book is the documentation of that statement. As you, the reader, work your way through the pages that follow, I think you will see that the documentation is so heavy, so complete, so thorough, and so weighty that it simply cannot be ignored or "explained away." Any **honest** inquirer will be able to quickly see that the students' charges are substantiated. They **have** been taught that Genesis 1-2 is a myth. They **have** been taught that evolution is factual. They **have** seen the Genesis account of creation attacked and belittled by men who are supposed to be—in a Christian university environment—upholding the word of God and teaching it as inspired and inerrant in every facet of composition. Instead, as the documentation which follows will show, some students have had their faith shaken by the open, flagrant teaching of modernistic concepts which strike at the very heart of the biblical record. Others, who have made valiant attempts to stand strong in the midst of such teachings, have suffered at the hands of some ACU professors and administrators. In one case a student's grade was lowered and his registration for further schooling was blocked. It is an ugly, ugly story which follows. How I wish it did not have to be told!

But it **must** be told. It must be told so that those members of the churches of Christ who have sacrificed (and who are still sacrificing) so that ACU may exist, will **know** what has happened, and what continues to be propagated within the sacred halls of one of "our" schools. It must be told so that parents and grandparents, uncles and aunts, and other family members will **know** what has occurred without their knowledge or consent. It must be told so that brethren will **know** that whereas we were once able to send our children to ACU with confidence that they would be taught the proper, biblical concept of their divine origin, such is no longer the case—at least in one academic department. It must be told so that brethren will **know** that ACU has violated its very charter—the bylaws upon which it was originally established—which pledge(s) it to teach the inspired, inerrant word of God without compromise in an atmosphere where our children will be both protected from error and instilled with a God-fearing respect for the Holy Scriptures. For all of these reasons—and more—the story you are about to read **must** be told.

Some, of course, will accuse us of unjust motives. Some will accuse us of bearing a grudge, or of "meddling" in matters that should not concern us. Some will accuse us of trying to "run the university." Some will accuse us of participating in a "witch-hunt." Some will accuse us of "quoting out of context." Some will accuse us of being rogues and scoundrels. Some will accuse us of having a "negative, unloving" attitude. Some will accuse us of. . . . Well, let us simply say that some already have!

And what shall we say to such accusations? We shall say simply this. Our love for ACU runs deep. But our love for the Truth of God runs even deeper. Error—whether it is taught in a one-on-one situation through mere ignorance—or whether it is taught publicly in an ACU biology classroom with prepared forethought, **must** be opposed. God did not give us an option regarding the opposition, publicly or privately, of error. We will not be deterred simply because some accuse us of "unloving" attitudes or "mean" spirits. We know our hearts, and can say without reservation that there is neither malice nor evil intent in our actions. In addition, we hasten to point out that the charges made here are by no means an indictment of the **entire** University community. There are, no doubt, many fine faculty members, and administration members, who perform their assigned tasks with dignity and success. Them we commend and applaud!

We will also say this. We have no desire to "run the university." We are perfectly content to leave that to University officials—**as long as they act in such a manner, and teach those**

things, which are consistent with the word of God. Should the time come (and indeed, it has) when certain ACU professors and/or administrators depart from teaching God's truth, and instead teach false, soul-damaging concepts that are nothing more than "the doctrines of men," let them clearly understand that we, and others among us who love both the University and the Bible, **will** oppose them. And that opposition has as its singular goal their repentance, and the return to the halls of ACU such teachings as place God in His proper perspective as Creator and Sustainer of the Universe, and Redeemer of fallen mankind!

Further, let it be clearly stated that we have no desire to participate in a "witch-hunt" of any kind. We are not searching daily for liberals and modernists under every bed or behind every rock. However, let it also be clearly stated that when error raises its ugly head, when liberals and modernists **do** assail the word of God, we **will**—like the prophets, apostles, and worthies of old—stand in opposition to them. Some among us seem to think that they can spout their error and blatant infidelity publicly, but then retreat behind some kind of "private, only-between-you-and-me" barricade when challenged. One would be hard-pressed to find a concept more at-odds with biblical teaching. **Public error demands public correction!** And so if some ACU professors are willing to **publicly** (in the classroom) call Genesis 1-2 a "myth"; if some are willing to call evolution a "fact accepted by all rational, thinking people"; if some are willing to belittle the facts of the divine creation account, then let it be duly noted that some among us will rise up in righteous indignation when the souls of our very children are endangered under the cloak of "academic freedom" or "higher education." There is no education higher than that given to our children as they are taught respect for, love for, and defense of the Truth of God! There is no "academic freedom" greater than being free to teach the "perfect law of liberty" to our children, unhindered by secular humanism and its godless concepts of evolution and man-made authority. Those involved in the teaching of error—who have been shown guilty by the documentation—have accused us of conducting a "witch-hunt," and "quoting out of context." Every false teacher we have ever known flees to the same "city of refuge." The charges will be proven to be false.

Wayne Jackson, in his "Introduction" to this volume, has commented that after reading the documentation herein contained, you may just wish to let ACU administrators "know how you feel." (Incidentally, I am indebted to my colleague and friend, Wayne Jackson, who has been apprised of this investigation since the beginning, and who has had access to all documents pertaining to this controversy. Wayne has made valuable editorial contributions to this book, and has assisted me in minor research and composition.) May I capitalize on his suggestion and urge you to do just that! As you will see from some statements of ACU administrators recorded in this book, the accountability of ACU to the brotherhood that supports it seems to be a thing of the past—at least in the eyes of some at ACU. I disagree! And I hope that every reader of these words will disagree as well! I hope that you will, upon reading this material, take the time to write ACU administrators, and **demand** an explanation of these matters. And I hope that you will be satisfied with nothing less than a full and complete explanation of how it is that certain professors can call Genesis 1-2 mythical, and evolution factual, and yet still retain their teaching positions at a "Christian" school. The University—all the disclaimers of some of its administrators and Board members notwithstanding—**is** accountable to our brotherhood. Let the sleeping giant quickly awake, **demand** that accountability, and seize this opportunity to let this school, and others if need be, know that we will **not** tolerate this flagrant denigration of the word of God. There **will be** an accounting! Let us make it now, rather than waiting for the great Day of Judgment yet to come. Souls—precious souls of our own young people—are very much at stake. God grant us the knowledge and determination to do that which is right, and the wisdom to realize the serious consequences of failing to act in accordance with His inspired commands.

Bert Thompson, Ph.D.
Montgomery, Alabama
January 1, 1986

PS: In an attempt to keep this booklet as small, and therefore as readable, as possible, with rare exceptions the reader will not see **extensive** refutation of such in-depth concepts as the Day-Age Theory, Gap Theory, and other aspects of evolution and/or theistic evolution. These refutations **are** found in the following books and are available from our offices: (1) *Theistic Evolution*; (2) *Essays In Apologetics* [Vol. I] ; (3) *The History of Evolutionary Thought*; (4) *The Scientific Case for Creation*, and; (5) *The Revelation of God in Nature*.

1

"In The Beginning..."

"Evolution's history and methodology will continue to feed debates for generations, but the fact of evolution is beyond dispute. The concept is rational, scientific, and supported by an overwhelming mass of evidence from past and present."
—Archie L. Manis
Elder, Baker Heights Church of Christ
Associate Professor of Biology, ACU
("Evolution Notes," p 3)

"Our teaching at ACU has more[1] presented evolution as an explanation for the world—it has been and is being presented as a body of scientific thought supported by a body of scientific evidence. As theory goes, there is no decisive evidence against any of these viewpoints from science."
—Archie L. Manis
(From his own handwritten explanation of his teaching of evolution at ACU, as presented to Mr. & Mrs. L.D. Swift, Tuscola, Texas, November, 1985, p 5.1)

The late, lamented Dr. Ira North, during his tenure as Editor of the *Gospel Advocate*, found it necessary on one particular occasion to both explain, and refute, a specific error being advocated throughout the brotherhood by various false

---
[1]See Appendix

teachers. The error, which was wide-spread and well-known amongst us, was of such a serious nature that allowing it to go unchecked would have caused immeasurable damage to the church of the living God. Dr. North full well knew that. Yet even though he knew that the error had to be quickly and effectively dealt with, he found his position—of having to be the one to expose the false teachers and refute their error—distasteful. Nevertheless, in the true spirit of every faithful editor of the "Old Reliable" who had gone before him, Ira North rose to the task and penned an editorial (accompanying almost an entire issue of the *Gospel Advocate* dealing with the error) which even to this day remains a classic. He entitled his editorial, "We Did Not Create, Originate or Instigate the Problem" (*Gospel Advocate*, May 24, 1979, p 322). His point—and it was well-made—was this: faithful members of the Lord's church had not **caused** the problem, and had not **taught** the error; rather, they were simply the ones who now found themselves having to refute the false teaching(s).

The title of that particular editorial comes forcefully to mind as we begin the task of preparing the material contained in this book. Truly, we did not "create, originate, or instigate the problem." But we, like Ira North and his faithful Assistant Editor, Guy N. Woods, find that we are face-to-face with false teachings that are fully as serious as those exposed by the editors of the *Gospel Advocate* in May of 1979. And while we want the reader to know that we, by no means, "created, originated, or instigated" the problem, we do not intend to merely ignore it. Our reasons for following the course of action now pursued are entirely scriptural.

It is **wrong** for Christians to ignore, be apathetic toward, or casual about false teachers and false teachings. It is **sinful** for Christians to allow false teachers to go unchallenged. It is **wrong** for Christians to tolerate false teachers and their teachings (II John 9-11). It is **wrong** for Christians to accept the teaching of and/or to extend Christian fellowship to false teachers (II John 10). The Scriptures still teach: "Now I beseech you, brethren, mark them that are causing the divisions and occasions of stumbling, contrary to the doctrine which ye learned: and turn away from them. For they that are such serve their own belly, and by their smooth and fair speech they beguile the hearts of the innocent" (Romans 16:17,18). Jude's **command** is that we ". . .contend earnestly for the faith which was once for all delivered unto the saints" (Jude 3). Paul's **command** is to "withdraw yourselves from every brother that walketh disorderly and not after the tradition which they received of us" (II Thessalonians 3:6). The Greek word which is translated "disorderly" is an adverbial form of the Greek verb *atakteo*, which Thayer says is a word used "of soldiers marching out of order, or quitting the ranks." The material contained in this book concerns men who are now known to be "wresting the Scriptures to their own destruction" (II Peter 3:16) and who, unashamedly, urge that others—particularly students under their tutelage—yield to their teaching. Most definitely this material is about men who are now—and apparently have been for quite some time—"marching out of order" because they no longer respect the testimony of God as expressed in His written word.

And so, while it is true that we did not "create, originate, or instigate" the problem, we will not ignore it. It is of such a magnitude—and apparently of such a longstanding nature—that it threatens, quite literally, to affect the lives and souls of hundreds, or even thousands, of young people. So, like Paul, we find ourselves "set for the defense of the Gospel" (Philippians 1:16) because we have no choice in the matter. Those who boldly step forward to compromise the plain teaching of the inspired word of God need to know that their attempted compromise(s) will **not** go unchallenged! Kindly, but ever so firmly, some among us **will** step forward to defend the "Old Jerusalem Gospel" for which our Lord lived—and died!

On February 25, 1985 a letter—from a young man who was (and is) a student at Abilene Christian University—arrived in our offices. The letter was dated February 22, 1985, and was written by Mark Scott. The letter told a story that was indeed incredible, and, as we thought at the time, almost unbelievable. Briefly stated, Mark wrote to request our help in a most serious matter. His letter (which is reproduced below) stated in no uncertain terms that certain professors in the biology department at Abilene Christian University were teaching, **as fact** organic and/or theistic evolution. Mark even named the two professors: Dr. Archie Manis, and Dr. Kenneth Williams.

The letter which we received, and the charges which that letter made, are as follows:

"Dear Dr. Thompson:

"My name is Mark Scott, and I am a biology major at Abilene Christian University. I understand you also were a biology major at Abilene.

"Evolution is being pushed on the students here at Abilene, by two teachers anyway, Archie Manis and Kenneth Williams. Manis teaches a Seminar In Biology class (actually, it ought to be called Seminar In **Evolution** because that is what it teaches and that alone). I wish it were called that, because I might not have come to Abilene if I had known a course on evolution would be required by biology majors. Manis has given us a textbook called *Science & Creationism*, edited by Montagu, copyright 1984, which he believes is the best, most important scientific work to come out since 1950 and that will destroy the Creationist view, and he believes the Creation Research Society will fold in the next few years. He says the purpose of the course is to expose us to Evolution, since most universities do the same, but he takes it much farther than that. Manis is an evolutionist, and gets upset when I would make comments in class opposing evolution, even though the seminar is a discussion-type class. He threatened to throw me out of class, the second day of class. As if the book isn't good enough in supporting evolution and trying to destroy creationism, he gives us lots of handouts supporting evolution. From handouts calling the Genesis account a myth and questioning the literal interpretation of Genesis—to handouts called 'The Case Against Creationism' and 'The Origin of Species' excerpts.

"He has even written me a letter saying I am 'not ready for this experience' because I have not had a course in genetics, and says my 'reservations and objections are quite frankly, tired old territory to me. Bear with us and you shall see why during the course of the semester.' He ends the letter by saying, 'I'm allowing you to remain in the seminar, yet admitting to certain reservations, knowing that you really don't belong there but trusting that you will allow the experiences to be rewarding to you.' In other words, he believes I haven't been brainwashed in the Biology Department at Abilene yet, since this is my first semester at Abilene. I spent my first two years at Williamstown Bible College, and at Northeastern Christian Junior College as a biology major, where evolution was not taught or supported. Although he apologized for his harsh comments in his letter that he wrote on a paper of mine ('I'm impatient with bigotry and intolerant of intolerance'), he considers me closed-minded and I consider him the same. I assured him in his office that even if I had taken genetics, I would still believe the way I do, and then he said that I ought to drop the class, but of course I refused.

"After the second day in Williams' botany class, I asked him why he taught evolution and he practically kicked me out of his office and got upset like Manis, when a person discussed the subject with them. I know also of another person who was practically kicked out of the office when evolution was discussed with Williams, and another who was going to be a biology teacher and took Williams' botany class and quit after the first day because so much evolution was taught on the first day! This student had to change his major as a result, because botany is a requirement (it is he who suggested that I write you). And I know of others who have expressed concern and dissatisfaction in Williams' approach to evolution to him. All he says is just to stay in class and we will see what he means. Any direct questions concerning evolution in class are avoided by him. He just simply approaches evolution as a fact from day one, just like in the state schools.

"In Manis' seminar, the Bible is attacked from the word 'go,' over and over again. There is, of course, dissatisfaction from many of the students here, although few express their concerns with teachers and administration. Apparently quite a few complaints have been made to the Department Head, but nothing done about it. Many of us came to a Christian University because we wanted teaching in accordance with the Bible, not ungodly teaching shoved down our throat. I came here to learn biology, not evolution.

"This past week, I have brought the situation before Perry Reeves, Dean of the College, and brought other students to him explaining that, yes, we really are being taught evolution.

He has talked to these two teachers, but still I see no change, except that Williams might not use the word 'evolution.'

"Many non-biology majors are very surprised to find out evolution is taught and pushed here by some teachers. Those I have talked to in the faculty here get very tense and nervous when a complaint of evolution is brought before them. Reeves says though that this is the first time that documented evidence has been brought before him, with specifics concerning teachers.

"If you would like, or can, help us in any way, we would appreciate it. This is a real problem, with persecutions and evil influences being taught to these students every class period—that goes against our faith.

"I read your *Reason & Revelation*, and use some of the material in these in my comments to them, as I am thinking of doing a paper on Creationism and Evolution. I have an uncle who is also involved with apologetics, named _____.

"Keep up the good work!"

As the reader can easily see, the letter makes some very serious charges. And, quite frankly, this writer was not easily disposed to believe the charges, for several reasons. First, Abilene Christian University (ACU) is my alma mater. I graduated from the University (then known as Abilene Christian College) in 1971, with a B.S. degree in biology and a minor in chemistry. Second, having spent all of my adult life as a professor and educator, I know firsthand that sometimes a student can genuinely "misunderstand" something that the professor said, and therefore go away with a wrong impression of what the professor meant to convey. Third, it seemed absolutely inconceivable to me that what Mark Scott **claimed** to be happening could actually **be** happening at one of "our" Christian colleges. How a **Christian** college could allow professors in any of its science departments to advocate evolution (the definitions of the word "evolution" as we use it will be given presently) was simply beyond my imagination.

On February 26, 1985 (just one day after receiving Mark Scott's initial letter) I penned a two-page response to Mark. In my letter, I explained that I was not disposed to simply accept—on his word alone—the charges set forth in his letter. I told him that if the accusations of his letter could actually be **documented** to my complete satisfaction, then (and only then) would I investigate further, and possibly assist him in getting this matter corrected. I suggested that Mark send me whatever documentation he might have.

In the early days of March, the local mail carrier delivered to our offices a huge packet of materials. The return address on the package was that of Mark Scott at ACU. Upon opening the package, I found inside page after page after page of the **heaviest kind** of documentation (some of which will be photoreproduced below), establishing the charges. Only a few examples will be given at this point, because additional comments will be made in the text below regarding these documents.

The first item to catch my attention was the frontispiece, which had been photocopied, of the book which Dr. Archie Manis was requiring his students to use as their textbook in his biology seminar class during the spring of 1985. The book is edited by the famous evolutionist/humanist of Princeton University, Dr. Ashley Montagu, and is entitled, *Science and Creationism*. I happen to have a copy of this book in my personal library, because a majority of my work in the fields of Christian apologetics and Christian evidences has to do with the creation/evolution controversy. In fact, I spend almost every weekend of the year lecturing around the country on this very topic. So, Dr. Montagu's book was no stranger to me. It is, in fact, one of the most vehement, anti-God, anti-Bible, anti-religion, anti-creation books that I have ever seen. It contains chapters by such noted evolutionists as Dr. Stephen J. Gould, Dr. Gunther Stent, Dr. Isaac Asimov, *et al.* Especially noticeable was the "ACU Bookstore" sticker on the frontispiece—indicating that the student(s) had been required to purchase the book **from the ACU Bookstore itself!** How such a book can be used in a **Christian** college science classroom escapes me—unless, of course, the book was being employed **in order to refute the authors' claims**. But, as the reader will soon learn, exactly the opposite was the case. The book was, in fact, required reading for the students, and **no refutation of any kind was ever given of the book's blasphemous contents**.

Second, several handouts from both Drs. Manis and Williams caught my eye, not the least of which was material (as given to the students by Dr. Manis) from Dr. Douglas J. Futuyma's book, *Science On Trial*. In this 1983 copyright book, Dr. Futuyma, a well-known atheistic evolutionist, openly attacks the biblical account of creation for which the churches of Christ have long stood without waivering. Those of us who work in the creation/evolution controversy know full-well the contents of this book. One of the chapters (Chapter 10), is entitled, "Creationist Arguments." This particular chapter (pages 175-196 in the book) is a belittling, denigrating attack upon creationism, and an attempted "refutation" of the scientific arguments which creationists have used (and effectively, I might add) for years. Imagine my surprise upon discovering that it was **this very chapter** which Dr. Manis had photocopied and handed to his students for required reading in his biology seminar! Once again, of course, I wondered just **how** a professor in a **Christian** college could possibly do such a thing, unless the purpose was to refute the error. Again, such was **not** the case!

Also included in the handouts from Dr. Manis' seminar class was a chapter from the infamous book by Dr. Philip Kitcher (and published by the prestigious M.I.T. University Press, copyright 1982), *Abusing Science: The Case Against Creationism*. The first chapter in Dr. Kitcher's book (which, like the Montagu and Futuyma books, is blatantly anti-God, anti-religion, anti-creation, anti-Bible) is entitled, "Evolution for Everyone," and is an apologetic for organic evolution. In this particular chapter (pp 7-29 of the book), Dr. Kitcher presents the "evidences" for evolution, in what many believe is one of the strongest arguments ever made for organic evolution. Significantly, it was these pages which Dr. Manis handed to his students, as **required reading**! Along with these sheets, Dr. Manis also presented the now-famous publication by Dr. Norman D. Newell of the American Geological Institute, *Why Scientists Believe in Evolution*. This 1984 publication is a bold attempt on the part of evolutionary geologists to explain the so-called "evidences" for evolution, and to "refute" creationism. The pamphlet presents the evolutionary geologic timetable as **fact**, and discusses at great length the "fact" that "all reputable" scientists accept evolution as true. And, as if this were not enough, Dr. Manis also distributed to the students, and required them to read, one of Dr. Stephen J. Gould's essays from *Natural History*. The essay was entitled, "A Clock of Evolution," and was another of Dr. Gould's attempts to "prove" evolution—this time from comparative anatomy (similarity in structure among living organisms). Anyone even vaguely familiar with the current creation/evolution controversy is acquainted with Gould's writings. He is the fiery young apostle of evolution from Harvard who is most renowned for his stand as a committed Marxist. [NOTE: The reader is asked to remember Dr. Gould's name, as shortly in the text below you will see it again. One of the texts used by Dr. Archie Manis when he taught the biology seminar class in the spring of 1984 was a text written by Gould!]

Other handout materials were found in the package of materials submitted to us for examination. None of these, however, was so unsettling and discomforting as the two which are about to be described. The first of these was from Dr. Archie Manis' biology seminar class. Interestingly enough, the four-page handout was authored by Dr. Manis himself, and was entitled, "Evolution Notes." So that the reader may get the full impact of exactly what the ACU professors **are actually teaching**, the "Evolution Notes" are photographically reproduced below. The reader is urged to carefully examine the "Evolution Notes," and specifically point #14 on page three. Notice the statement which says that, "Evolution's history and methodology will continue to feed debates for generations, but the **fact** of evolution is beyond dispute. The concept is **rational, scientific, and supported by an overwhelming mass of evidence from past and present**" (emphasis added).

[See pages 10–13 for photoreproductions of Manis' "Evolution Notes."]

evolution notes

1. Charles Robert Darwin (1809-1882: he and Abraham Lincoln share a February 12 birthdate) read Thomas Malthus' 1798 essay on human populations in 1838. This sparked Darwin to conclude a conceptual scheme in the works for some time, mostly from 1831 to 1835 on HMS Beagle: natural selection leading to transmutation. The Origin of Species by Means of Natural Selection was released on 24 November 1859 (we usually read the sixth edition of 1872), 21 years after his idea was fully formed, and then only because Alfred Russell Wallace was about to publish the identical theory. Darwin's "The Descent of Man," in which the term "evolution" was used in a more or less modern sense, appeared in 1871. These two are the more famous of his many writings.

2. Gregor Mendel's laws were published in 1866 and independently rediscovered by researchers Carl Erich Correns, Erich Tschermak and Hugo DeVries in 1900. Mendel's work had been buried in an obscure journal, "The Proceedings of the Natural History Society of Brunn"--apparently Nageli was mostly to blame for that tragedy, but it is likely that Darwin himself failed to read Mendel's work though it lay among his papers for years.

3. The Scopes "Monkey Trial" in Dayton, Tennessee, happened during a sticky hot spell in the summer of 1925. A supreme court ruling in 1968 closed the issue that prompted the Scopes trial. In 1969 a California law rippled through the science textbook selection processes across the nation. A 1981 Arkansas "equal time" law was overturned in 1982. This trial was likely the most thorough and significant of its kind, and yet the issues around religion versus science keep resurrecting in educational and legislative circles.

4. One can never fully appreciate the conceptual scheme of evolution without mastering the profound law named for its discoverers (Hardy-Weinberg, 1908) who independently proposed the mathematical model that characterizes a hypothetical population as follows:
   A. Population composition: theoretically an infinitely large number of sexually reproducing diploids
   B. Mating is random, including random selfing; equal opportunity gametic unions
   C. Allele pairs all adaptively neutral: no selection for or against either allele; all genotypes possess equal viability and leave progeny in direct proportion to their respective frequencies
   D. Closed population: no organisms can get in or out
   E. Mutations do not occur
   F. Generation overlap does not occur
   G. Population members are equal in reproductive age
   H. Chance is the sole determiner in gametogenesis and in allele segregation; meiosis is exclusively normal

            I. Males and females have equal gene frequencies
            J. Parents contribute equally to heredity of offspring
   The consequence of this Hardy-Weinberg law is genetic
   equilibrium. Allelic frequencies of the gene pool and
   genotype distribution remain constant generation to generation,
   if the restrictions apply.

5. Evolution results when these Hardy-Weinberg restrictions are
   compromised. Populations in nature are not infinitely large,
   random mating probably never happens, mutations do occur, etc.
   In nature, the restrictions probably never apply. Thus
   evolution is the inevitable process whereby changes in the gene
   pool, nonrandom shifts in gene frequency, are affected.

6. The gene pool, in the opinion of many biologists, is the most
   basic evolutionary unit. Ernst Mayr says, "species are groups
   of interbreeding natural populations that are reproductively
   isolated from other such groups." What is your species concept?
   Reproductive isolating mechanisms are prezygotic (ecological,
   temporal, behavioral, mechanical, gametic) and postzygotic
   (hybrid inviability, hybrid sterility, hybrid breakdown).

7. Dollo's law states that evolution along any specific lineage is
   essentially irreversible; feral groups respond to natural
   selection by reverting toward a phenotype that resembles their
   ancestral forms (atavism). It is possible, in theory, for an
   ancestral duplication to occur, but it's most unlikely.

8. Extinction has been the fate of most species, by phyletic
   replacement or (more often) by leaving no descendants, as in
   the dinosaur extinction at the close of the Cretaceous period.

9. Dendritic or branching (bush-like) schematics depict evolutionary
   divergence; after geographic speciation, or the faster quantum
   speciation (involving hybridization, which includes
   allopolyploidy and introgression in plants) the cladogram
   becomes net-like, with arms.

10. Evolution is often retrogressive or degenerative, and evolutionary
    rates vary considerably.

11. Cope's law states that evolution tends to produce larger (not more
    complex, but larger; read closely) organisms. It was first
    observed in vertebrates, then in invertebrates and plants.

12. Darwin's revolutionary contribution to human knowledge, natural
    selection, incorporates these concepts:
       A. Populations display tremendous variety,
       B. There is a tendency to overpopulate,
       C. Offspring which adapt and reproduce are successful; they
          survive more efficiently than others,
       D. Subsequent generations exhibit nonrandom shifts in gene
          frequencies, which is the natural consequence of
          adaptation, the organism's (collectively, not individually;
          we're talking about a population) response to nature's
          selection pressures. Natural selection is not only a
          weeding-out of the unfit, but also a creator of fitter

organisms. Natural selection sorts and salvages; it selects the relatively few adaptive gene combinations from multitudes of less fit possibilities. The role of natural selection as evolution's primal force was not fully appreciated until the 1940's.

13. Statistical methods and population genetics sprang from the 1920's and 1930's. Oparin (Russia) and Haldane (England) speculated about early earth in 1929. H.B.D. Kettlewell and his Oxford University group offered elegant proof of natural selection using Biston betularia and B. carbonaria, the peppered moth, in 1952-1959.

14. Neo-Darwinism (gradualism) and punctuated equilibrium (S.J. Gould and N. Eldredge, 1970's, perhaps traceable to Karl Wilhelm Von Nageli's "jumps" in an 1884 book; Mendel had sent his 1866 paper to Nageli, who failed to see its significance and was largely responsible for its lack of notice in the scientific community) provide today's biologist a variety of theoretical options in the evolution of evolution, as it were. Evolution's history and methodology will continue to feed debates for generations; but the fact of evolution is beyond dispute. The concept is rational, scientific, and supported by an overwhelming mass of evidence from past and present.

15. The new geology rocketed out of the early 1970's, built on familiar notions like an ancient earth, and newer ones like plate tectonics; sea-floor spreading, and continental drift. Data from ship and satellite profoundly altered man's understanding of his planet (the Soviets' beeping little Sputnik had launched the U.S. space program in October, 1957; U.S. astronauts walked on the moon in 1969). Modern biology and modern geology together unveiled a grand picture. Now more than ever before, we envisage evolution as it is, the quite blind, purposeless, nonprogressive, certain process that fitfully yields "descent with modification"--resolutely proclaiming a plastic heredity responding to varying environmental pressures, from geologic change, from time's relentless grind. Evolution is the curious mix of caprice and selection, the workings of nature in her essential creative enterprise.

16. Religious men of Judeo-Christian tradition have dealt misery to those whose ideas opposed theirs. Remember Copernicus? The man had the cheek to tell the people that their earth was not at the center of everything, so they made him pay. Him and anyone else who'd believe that stuff, and for very good religious reasons. So there. Now the creationists don't like being compared with those people, not all that far removed from the historical present, but the analogy has been drawn. The adamant creationists would have everyone believe that their objections to evolution models are valid for both religious and scientific reasons. The scientists object to that, cogently protesting that "creation science" is not science, just religion in disguise. Ain't it fun!

17. From A.E. Carlson (Human Genetics, Heath, 1984, p. 408): Human values had changed dramatically long before Darwin was

born. We no longer believe, as we once did, universally, that
government is the divine right of kings. Nor do we condone
capital punishment for witchcraft, blasphemy, or heresy. We no
longer believe that disease is a punishment for individual or
collective lapses of morality or piety.

Meaning and purpose in human life are found among theists,
atheists, and agnostics. It is the burden and the
responsibility of all human beings to seek those values, whether
from the tenets of a specific religion or from the experience
and wisdom of our past and present cultures. Neo-Darwinism will
neither destroy not provide the need for values, but it does
force us to expand our views of life, time, and the human
condition.

18. Refer to the "Research in Genesis" handout.

Imagine, if you can, a professor from a **Christian** college or university authoring a class handout which blatantly calls evolution a "fact" that is "rational, scientific, and supported by an overwhelming mass of evidence"?! It is doubtful that anything else would be needed to establish the claims that indeed, evolution **is** being taught as "fact" to students in the biology department at ACU. But, as incredible as that is, there is **more**!

The single most outrageous handout was not, in fact, authored by Dr. Archie Manis, but was instead authored by God Himself. However, what made the "handout" so repulsive was the fact that Dr. Manis, in a bold stroke of self-aggrandizement, flying directly in the face of biblical commands against adding to or taking from the inspired word of God, took it upon himself to write—in the margin of a photocopy of the text of Genesis 1—that the account was a "myth"!! In order that the reader may actually see for himself exactly how bold Dr. Manis is, that handout is photographically reproduced below. Examine closely—in Dr. Manis' own handwriting—the word "myth" beside Genesis 1. Note also how Manis terms the creation account a "hymn."

[See pages 15–16 for photoreproductions of Manis' "Research in Genesis."]

RESEARCH IN GENESIS

Carefully read the Genesis account of Creation as told in chapters one and two of the Bible. I recommend that you use several committee versions, such as: American Standard, Revised Standard, New English, New American Standard, and New International. You may want to use the King James Version also, but expect some difficulty with the English of the older versions, like the KJV and the ASV. Search the scriptures, commentaries, and lexicons for answers to these questions (don't hesitate to ask a reference librarian, for example, to help you find good materials):

(1) When was "the beginning" of Genesis 1:1?

(2) Precisely what was "the light" of Genesis 1:3?

(3) Comment on "evening and morning, one day" in Genesis 1:5 and other verses.

(4) Describe the "firmament" of Genesis 1:8.

(5) Describe the sequence of creation events recorded in Genesis 1, day by day; list the items and the "creation day" given for each one.

(6) Describe the sequence of creation events recorded in Genesis 2:4-25, day by day; list the items and the "creation day" given for each one.

(7) Discuss the differences between the two "creation hymns" (5 and 6 above). Are these two accounts of the same creation story, or is this repetition with a change in sequence?

(8) Give a modern definition of "day"; base your definition on astronomy, and tell me what you found out about any changes in day length, looking back through earth history.

(9) How were "days" measured before the sun (Genesis 1:16)? How long were these "days"? Document the various uses of the word translated "day" elsewhere in the Bible: what lengths of time does "day" cover?

Here are some English words that have been used to translate certain Hebrew expressions. List the verses in chapters one and two of Genesis where these Hebrew terms are found, and supply a lexicon definition for each Hebrew term (commentaries often give excellent definitions, but use the lexicons directly if you can): (1) fruit (1:11), (2) seed (1:11), (3) kind (1:21), (4) created (1:1, 27), (5) made (1:16) or make (1:26); (6) day (1:5). Were "create" and "make" both used in connection with the origin of man? Was the word translated "create" ever translated "made" or "make" elsewhere in scripture? Which term actually applies to the origin of man?

You also need to present a carefully written, documented or annotated statement of the modern, synthetic view of evolution. Include a discussion of plate tectonics, sea floor spreading, and continental drift. Finally, synthesize these two studies into a personal statement of belief about origins.

I'm sure you will profit from this research, and I'm looking forward to reading your papers! Be sure they are well documented (utilize recognized, scholarly, recent sources), and written in an appropriate, accepted style.

Archie L. Manis, Ph.D.
Abilene Christian University
15 March 1983

Creation
Hymn, Myth #1 → 1:1-2:3
Hymn, Myth #2 → 2:4-24

The First Book of Moses

Commonly Called

Genesis

(RSV)

1:27 Creates man and woman? (male, female)
2:7 forms man
2:21-22 makes woman
3:17 "Adam" = man (generic)
3:20 "Eve" ~ mother

#1

1 In the beginning God created* the heavens and the earth. ²The earth was without form and void, and darkness was upon the face of the deep; and the Spirit* of God was moving over the face of the waters.

DAY 1
heavens
earth
light
day
night

3 And God said, "Let there be light"; and there was light. ⁴And God saw that the light was good; and God separated the light from the darkness. ⁵God called the light Day, and the darkness he called Night. And there was evening and there was morning, one day.

DAY 2
firmament

6 And God said, "Let there be a firmament in the midst of the waters, and let it separate the waters from the waters." ⁷And God made the firmament and separated the waters which were under the firmament from the waters which were above the firmament. And it was so. ⁸And God called the firmament Heaven. And there was evening and there was morning, a second day.

DAY 3
land & plants

9 And God said, "Let the waters under the heavens be gathered together into one place, and let the dry land appear." And it was so. ¹⁰God called the dry land Earth, and the waters that were gathered together he called Seas. And God saw that it was good. ¹¹And God said, "Let the earth put forth vegetation, plants yielding seed, and fruit trees bearing fruit in which is their seed, each according to its kind, upon the earth." And it was so. ¹²The earth brought forth vegetation, plants yielding seed according to their own kinds, and trees bearing fruit in which is their seed, each according to its kind. And God saw that it was good. ¹³And there was evening and there was morning, a third day.

DAY 4
lights
sun
moon
stars

14 And God said, "Let there be lights in the firmament of the heavens to separate the day from the night; and let them be for signs and for seasons and for days and years, ¹⁵and let them be lights in the firmament of the heavens to give light upon the earth." And it was so. ¹⁶And God made the two great lights, the greater light to rule the day, and the lesser light to rule the night; he made the stars also. ¹⁷And God set them in the firmament of the heavens to give light upon the earth, ¹⁸to rule over the day and over the night, and to separate the light from the darkness. And God saw that it was good. ¹⁹And there was evening and there was morning, a fourth day.

20 And God said, "Let the waters bring forth swarms of living creatures, and let birds fly above the earth across the firmament of the heavens." ²¹So God created the great sea monsters and every living creature that moves, with which the waters swarm, according to their kinds, and every winged bird according to its kind. And God saw that it was good. ²²And God blessed them, saying, "Be fruitful and multiply and fill the waters in the seas, and let birds multiply on the earth." ²³And there was evening and there was morning, a fifth day.

24 And God said, "Let the earth bring forth living creatures according to their kinds: cattle and creeping things and beasts of the earth according to their kinds." And it was so. ²⁵And God made the beasts of the earth according to their kinds and the cattle according to their kinds, and everything that creeps upon the ground according to its kind. And God saw that it was good.

26 Then God said, "Let us make man in our image, after our likeness; and let them have dominion over the fish of the sea, and over the birds of the air, and over the cattle, and over all the earth, and over every creeping thing that creeps upon the earth." ²⁷So God created man in his own image, in the image of God he created him; male and female he created

*Or When God began to create *Or wind
1.1: Jn 1.1.
1.26, 27: Gen 5.1; Mt 19.4; Mk 10.6, Col 3.10, Jas 3.9.

The package of materials sent for our examination contained more—much more, in fact, than there is room here to mention. Dr. Manis also handed out photocopies of Charles Darwin's "Conclusion" to the sixth edition of his *Origin of Species*. Dr. Williams reproduced on overhead transparencies materials "explaining" how "factual" the geologic timetable was, and how that "evolution" accounted for the entirety of the plant kingdom. Dr. Manis authored a two-page document which he called "Research in Genesis," which contained some nine major points. In that listing of points, #7 stated, "Discuss the differences between the two 'creation hymns. . . .'" This statement is obviously an allusion to the modernist notion that Genesis 1 and 2 are divergent documents later combined by some unknown redactor. Other points called into question the "days" of Genesis as being literal 24-hour days, and suggested, quite strongly, that the "wording" of Genesis 1 is simply "not understandable" to the twentieth century Christian— a disgusting reflection upon the Author of the Scriptures!

Upon seeing these materials—and many more which space forbids including, there was but one conclusion to draw. The conclusion was that the charges which had been levelled against the two professors were proven beyond any shadow of doubt! In fact, in all of my years dealing with both evolutionists and theistic evolutionists, I have yet to see such a strong case documenting the teaching of error as this material contained. But, I hasten to add, it was not a conclusion which I **wanted** to reach. In fact, as I have already mentioned, I had good reasons for **not** wanting to reach this particular conclusion. I found it difficult to admit to myself that my own alma mater—the school which I dearly loved—was involved in such ungodly activities as represented by the false teachings herein described. It was a sad day indeed when that package of materials arrived in my office. For, now that I **knew** of the error being advocated, I simply could not turn my back and walk away. As I have already made clear from the Scriptures, it is **wrong** for a Christian to ignore false doctrine. It is **wrong** for a Christian to allow false teachers to go unchallenged and unexposed. It is even more detestable to attempt a cover-up of error! The burden which once belonged to others, was now mine as well. And it was a burden not to be enjoyed!

As I sifted, ever-so-slowly, through the mountain of materials which the two professors were using to teach evolution as factual, still more documents reached my office. Yet another ACU student, Kent West, wrote us a letter dated March 13, 1985. The story told was equally shocking. Kent's first paragraph stated that he had heard that Mark Scott had written to us complaining about the teaching of evolution, **as fact**, at ACU, and that he wanted to "put in his two cents." Kent's letter stated, in part, as follows:

"...I was absolutely thrilled to have the chance to go to a Bible-supporting Christian college, and hear the other wise (creationist) for a welcome change. What a royal disappointment! I expressed my disappointment and anger to my adviser, who suggested I pursue it and talk to the higher-ups. I now regret that I never did. I started out my first semester at ACU enrolled in Astronomy and Plant Taxonomy. The first day in Plant Tax, I decided I wanted out. The instructor (Dr. Kenneth Williams) said he believed in evolution (at least among plants). He also made several references to the geologic timescale as fact and wanted us to learn it. ....I dropped that class. I went to ACU to hear the creationist side. I was not about to take anymore if I could help it, and I sure wasn't going to pay to hear it. I was really irked. I changed my major from life-earth sciences for two reasons: (1) I was more interested in earth sciences and ACU's emphasis was very predominately life-sciences; (2) If ACU was going to teach evolution, I did not want to be educated by that school in those fields. If it weren't for the evolutionary teaching, I probably would have stayed with that major. As I mentioned, I was also enrolled in Astronomy. I went ahead and stayed in that class. What did I learn? The course was a course in stellar evolution. I didn't really have that much of a qualm with the observations and interpretations of what is going in space **now**, but it bothered me a great deal that the instructor was strongly evolutionary (theistic, of course) in his cosmogony. I stopped by his office one day and talked for a while. If I remember correctly, he interpreted the early chapters of Genesis as figurative in some way. . . .What?! A Christian college that teaches the Bible to be allegorical when the evidence points otherwise? There goes my naivete. . . .Maybe this will give you some idea of what is going on at ACU. . . .Keep up the good work at Apologetics Press. God Almighty be with you!

(signed) Kent West"

Then, on April 1, 1985 **still another** letter arrived from yet **another** student. In the first draft of the book you are now reading, a lengthy quotation from this student's letter was given. However, on November 29, 1985, we received a letter from the student, asking us to please not mention his name or use any quotations from his letter. We, of course, respected his request, and removed the quotation from the book. One cannot help but wonder, of course, why the student had such a change of heart? His original letter was quite specific in recalling what had happened in the classes he had taken under one of these two professors, as he spelled out how evolution is taught exactly as presented in the evolutionary textbooks, and offered **without refutation** or presentation of any scientific and/or biblical evidences supporting the creation account. Now, however, that students are learning about how Mark Scott has been treated, and as they learn that the cover-up is about to be made public, it appears as though they are afraid to state the facts as they know them. Or, is it possible that ACU administrators are pressuring students to retract accusatory statements made earlier in all good conscience? In either case, the effect is the same. And it does not complement those at ACU. As we have pointed out before, intimidation is the name of the game.

The time to act had come. The unsupported accusations of a single student might have been ignored, but the evidence had now grown far beyond that, as several factors reveal.First, Mark Scott is not a novice; he is a 25-year old senior. Second, there were other corroborating witnesses. Third, the evidences

from the professors themselves told the entire story whether there were any student witnesses or not! [NOTE: This point is crucial. As the reader will presently note, ACU administrative officials are now labeling Mark Scott as a "troublemaker," attempting to discredit his story. To that we reply: what else would one **expect** them to call him?? After all, he was the one who first brought their many errors to light in what can now be documented as a full **decade** of such false teaching! In addition, we assert that the issue does not center around Mark Scott at all. He just happened to be the first of several students to contact us. The case stands on its own merits, without Scott's testimony one way or the other.] The professors' personal handouts (including a handwriting notation of Genesis 1 as "myth") have indicted them—and they are guilty as charged!

———◇◇◇———

Confronting The Professors

"Meaning and purpose in human life are found among theists, atheists, and agnostics. It is the burden and the responsibility of all human beings to seek those values, whether from the tenets of a specific religion or from the experience and wisdom of our past and present cultures. Neo-Darwinism will neither destroy nor provide the need for values, but it does force us to expand our views of life, time, and the human condition."

—Archie L. Manis
Elder, Baker Heights Church of Christ
Associate Professor of Biology, ACU
("Evolution Notes," p 4)

With massive amounts of evidence now before us, and with sincere pleas from concerned students weighing on our hearts, there was but one thing to do. The students' testimonies had been heard, the professors' statements had been duly examined, and the only possible conclusion which could be drawn had been drawn. The time was now ripe to approach—on an individual basis—the two professors in order to ask **why** such was happening. Was there **any** explanation which could cause some other conclusion to be drawn? On March 27, 1985 I wrote personal letters to each of the two professors involved, Drs. Archie Manis and Kenneth Williams. The letters were sent by certified mail with a return receipt, so that we would **know** that the two professors did, in fact, receive them. No one else at the University was sent a copy of either letter. The biology department head, Dr. John Little, did not receive a copy. The Dean of the College of Natural and Applied Sciences, Dr. Perry Reeves, did not receive a copy. Only the two professors who were directly involved received copies of the letters. We wanted each of these professors to have an opportunity to **privately** and **personally** answer our letters, without any involvement of upper-level ACU administrators. We felt this was only fair. The letters, as sent to the two professors on March 27, 1985, are reproduced below. Dr. Manis' letter is reproduced in its entirety; Dr. Williams' letter is reproduced only in the sections that differed from the Manis letter (portions of the two letters were exactly the same; those sections have been omitted to save space in this publication). The reader will note that appended to each letter was a listing of questions, the purpose of which was to see what the two professors **did**, in fact, believe. The reader is urged to examine the questions carefully. They represent "basics" among us, and are questions that any Christian—who has nothing to hide—should be able to answer, and should have no hesitation in answering. The quibble has been made, however, that the questions were "trick" questions. However, Dr. Furman Kearley, who was at that time Professor of Bible and Director of Graduate Bible Studies at ACU (but who has since left the University), when asked by Dr. C.G. Gray, Vice-President for Academic Affairs, to examine the questions, dashed off the answers in approximately ten minutes, and said, "What's the problem? Get the two professors to answer the questions." Enough said!

"Dear Dr. Manis:

"I send you greetings from those of us associated with the work of Apologetics Press, Inc.

"I am writing regarding a matter of great concern to me. As you may be aware, I am an alumnus of Abilene Christian University, having received my B.S. degree in biology from ACU while Dr. Clark Stevens was chairman of the Department of Biology. In fact, because of Dr. Stevens' encouragement, and due in part to his efforts on my behalf, I made the decision to attend graduate school at Texas A&M University, where I was accepted and later graduated after having completed both my M.S. and Ph.D. degrees in food microbiology. Upon my graduation from Texas A&M, I taught for several years in the College of Veterinary Medicine at Texas A&M. Currently, I am a Professor of Bible and Science at the Alabama Christian School of Religion here in Montgomery, under the direction of Dr. Rex A. Turner, Sr. I mention these things so that you will know something of my background and scholastic training, and so that you will understand my 'special' interest in Abilene Christian University. I hold my alma mater in high regard, and always have. I also mention these things so that you will know that I am writing to you not only as a concerned alumnus, but as a fellow scientist as well.

"Dr. Manis, I have spent most of my adult life studying in the areas of Christian apologetics and Christian evidences. Because of my scientific training, a special area of interest to me is the creation/evolution controversy. I have studied many years in this particular area, am familiar with the renowned evolutionists of both the past and of our day, and make it a point to 'keep current' regarding the present controversy. In addition, I speak almost every weekend of the year on the creation/evolution problem (in an attempt to help people see the paucity of evolutionary theory and the threat it represents to the Christian faith), and have written several books, chapters in books, and monographs dealing with creation and evolution. Again, I say all of this so that you will have some idea of the background from which I am writing.

"With those prefatory remarks complete, let me now turn my full attention to the reason for this particular letter. As I have indicated, I am writing regarding a matter of great concern to me, both as an alumnus of Abilene Christian University, and as a Christian (and scientist) who understands the logical implications of the acceptance of evolution. [NOTE: At the outset, let me make the definitions of my terms clear to you. When I employ the word 'evolution,' I am discussing the General Theory of Evolution, i.e., organic evolution as the term is generally employed in the scientific community.]

"In recent weeks, I have received telephone calls and letters from some at Abilene Christian who are students in your class, and in another professor's class, in the biology department. The purpose of these calls and letters by the students was to request assistance from those of us here at Apologetics Press, Inc. Our work is fairly well-known, and our materials are quite wide-spread. Some of the students had seen some of our materials, and called or wrote to inquire about securing additional materials, and advice, on how to deal with a specific problem they were having in these specific biology classes at ACU.

"Their 'problem' in some of their biology classes at ACU was, as they explained in great detail, this: they are being taught evolution in certain classes and, in fact, have even been in some classes (yours specifically) where evolution is not only taught, but where the Genesis account of creation is both belittled and ridiculed. My first reaction upon hearing these accusations was, of course, incredulity. This situation, where professors of biology at a **Christian** college or university would not only teach and advocate as factual organic evolution, but openly and boldly call the creation account of Genesis a 'myth,' sits oddly upon an institution which is supposed to be known for instilling faith in our children in **every** area of academic endeavor, whether it be science, Bible, or physical education. 'Cramming evolution down the students' throats' (to use one student's exact words) is hardly a faith-building endeavor, to say the very least! If the accusations are true, the damage to a young person's faith could hardly be **over**estimated!

"Upon hearing the students' complaints, two things were foremost in my mind. First, it was apparent to me that I should, as a Christian, give the professors involved the benefit of the doubt. As a professor, I know that sometimes a student may simply misunderstand or misinterpret something that was said in class, perhaps due to the fact that the student was unfamiliar with the concept or because he simply didn't have the 'whole picture' at that point in time. Second, I felt that I should not be hasty in forming any conclusion(s) regarding these accusations until I had proper evidence upon which to base such conclusions. Having been trained in research, I know full well the importance of first seeking out the facts before reaching any conclusions. Consequently, I set about to gather evidence which would help me to reach whatever conclusion(s) that evidence demanded. I wrote letters, made phone calls, made contact with some of the students, etc. Only after painstaking efforts on my part, and only after seeing in written form the materials which come to bear on this matter, have I decided to write you this letter.

"Dr. Manis, I have here in my office materials which you are using in your seminar class at Abilene Christian University, as well as materials which are being used by at least one other professor in the biology department. After examining in great depth these materials, there is but one conclusion which I can reach, and that conclusion is that the accusations which have been levelled against you are correct and true. To be quite honest, I had trouble believing that such materials as you are using in your class(es) would ever be found on a Christian college campus, except possibly to refute them. But to take such materials and make them the basis of a class, in order to both advocate organic evolution and to belittle the Genesis account of creation, I find deplorable!

"One or two examples will certainly suffice. When the students informed me that you were using as your seminar textbook the book, *Science and Creationism*, edited by Dr. Ashley Montagu, I could not believe it. I know all too well of Dr. Montagu, and this particular book. Dr. Montagu is the re-nowned humanist/evolutionist who recently went on record as stating that 'absolute truth belongs only to one class of hu-mans. . .the class of absolute fools' (*The Atlanta Journal and Constitution*, 7-26-81, p 4-C). Dr. Montagu's aversion to the Bible, God, and related matters is too well-documented to need comment. And anyone even vaguely familiar with evolution and its adherents in humanism today would recognize the 'who's who' of humanistic/evolutionary thought that were contributors to the book which Dr. Montagu edited (and which you are using in your attempts to present evolution and re-fute creationism). The names of men like Isaac Asimov, Stephen Jay Gould, Gunther Stent, and Garrett Hardin are well-known to those of us who are constantly in the battle against humanism and its system of evolutionary origins. Upon receiving a large packet of materials to document the students' claims, and upon seeing the photocopy of the frontispiece from the Montagu book, I picked up the phone (again, to give you the benefit of the doubt) and telephoned one of the students to ask if it was possible that you were simply using the book as an 'example' of evolutionary thought, in order to refute the claims made in the book. This particular student said that it was quite the reverse—the claims of the book against creationism, and the God behind creation, were being vindicated in class. The student said that in order to convince me, copies of handouts used in your seminar class could be sent. They **were** sent, and I have them sitting here in my office as I write you this letter. I am amazed and appalled at what I see. One of the handouts, authored by you, is entitled 'Research in Genesis.' Attached to it is a photocopy of the first page of the Bible, containing Genesis 1. Out beside the biblical text, in the margin, are your markings to the students. When I read out beside Genesis 1:1 your comment that it was a 'hymn' or 'creation myth,' I was left speechless. How a professor in a **Christian** college or university, much less my own alma mater, could advocate such was beyond my comprehension.

"The documentation which I have received certainly speaks for itself. I have never seen such a motley assortment of anti-creationist materials in a Christian college environment before. From your photocopied handout (given to the students) of material from Philip Kitcher's recent book, *Abusing Science: The Case Against Creationism*, to your own 'Evolution Notes,' these materials represent some of the most venemous materials I have ever come across. For me to be presented with the fact that such materials are being used at my own alma mater, to undermine the faith of precious young minds, causes me a grief which I cannot adequately express to you in this letter!

"Dr. Manis, the purpose of this letter is two-fold. First, I am writing you to ask an explanation of these ongoings. As an alumnus of the University, as a former student in the very department where these things are being taught, and as a brother in the Lord, I feel I have every right to inquire regarding these matters. I do not have to tell you by now that I am **very** disturbed at the documentation I have seen. The students' charges have been proven true by the very information which has been presented in class. There is no doubt that an explanation from you is in order. I, personally, would appreciate one. No doubt, others would as well. Second, I am writing to provide you an opportunity to respond to these allegations. If I have 'misunderstood,' then this letter is my request that you help me to properly understand. If you feel that some of the documentation was inappropriate, then this letter will provide you with an opportunity to correct that as well.

"In an attempt to better understand exactly what you **do** believe regarding these matters, and to properly and correctly understand what you **are** teaching, I am asking you to please provide me with answers to the questions which you will find listed below. These are questions which any Christian ought to be able to answer quickly and easily, as they represent 'basics' among us. They are intended to elicit simply a 'yes' or 'no' answer; however, should you feel that more is needed, please do not hesitate to append whatever response you feel is justified. I will eagerly await your response, as I am anxious to see a solution to this problem, which is affecting the faith of young people under your tutelage, and at **my** alma mater. I deem this to be a problem of no little significance, and I wish you to know that I would like to do everything humanly possible to ensure that the situation as it is now stands does not continue.

Sincerely,
(signed) Bert Thompson, Ph.D.
Professor of Bible & Science
Alabama Christian School of Religion

"Attachment

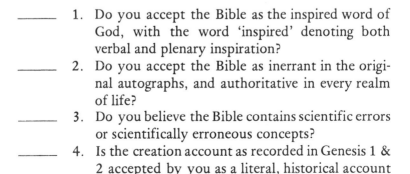

_____ 1. Do you accept the Bible as the inspired word of God, with the word 'inspired' denoting both verbal and plenary inspiration?

_____ 2. Do you accept the Bible as inerrant in the original autographs, and authoritative in every realm of life?

_____ 3. Do you believe the Bible contains scientific errors or scientifically erroneous concepts?

_____ 4. Is the creation account as recorded in Genesis 1 & 2 accepted by you as a literal, historical account of God's creation of the universe and the life forms in that universe?

_____ 5. Do you accept Genesis 1-11 as literal and historical (i.e., as opposed to being 'mythical' or 'allegorical,' etc.)?

_____ 6. Do you consider the creation account as told in Genesis 1 & 2 to be merely a 'hymn' or 'myth' as opposed to a literal, historical account?

_____ 7. Is the General Theory of Evolution (i.e., organic evolution) basically correct as an explanation for the various life forms which now exist or have existed?

_____ 8. Does the General Theory of Evolution (i.e., organic evolution) contradict the biblical account of origins?

_____ 9. Is theistic evolution (or progressive creation) acceptable to you? That is to say, do you believe in both God and organic evolution?

_____ 10. Are the days during which creation occurred (as discussed in Genesis 1, Exodus 20:11, Exodus 31:17, et. al.) accepted by you as being literal days of approximately 24-hours each?

_____ 11. Do you believe the creation days (discussed in question #10 above) to be possibly long periods of time rather than normal days of approximately 24-hours each?

_____ 12. Is the standard evolutionary geologic timetable an essentially correct explanation of the history of life on earth, in your estimation?

_____ 13. Do you believe that the Bible allows for a creation of life forms of any kind prior to the creation week as discussed in Genesis 1?

_____ 14. Do you accept evolutionary estimates of the age of the earth/universe which attempt to establish the earth/universe as having ages measured in billions of years?

_____ 15. Do you believe that the Bible allows for a multi-billion year old earth/universe?

_____ 16. If your answer to question #15 above is 'yes,' where in the biblical account of creation would you place these long time spans? Please place the letter in the blank at the left of the appropriate answer:

    (A) **Before** the creation week?

    (B) **During** the creation week?

    (C) **After** the creation week?

_____ 17. In your estimation, may a faithful child of God accept, teach, and promulgate the General Theory of Evolution (i.e., organic evolution)?

_____ 18. In your estimation, may a faithful child of God accept **both** a naturalistic **and** supernaturalistic view of the origin of the universe and all life forms in that universe, and still be acceptable to God?

_____ 19. Do you teach theistic evolution (i.e., that the theory of evolution as taught in most scientific circles today may be accepted at the same time as belief in God) in your classes at Abilene Christian University?

_____ 20. Are you handing out to the students in any of your classes written materials which suggest or teach, directly or indirectly, that the General Theory of Evolution (i.e., organic evolution) is correct and true, and to be accepted?

_____ 21. Are you refuting the General Theory of Evolution (i.e., organic evolution) in your classes, in an attempt to make certain that your students understand it is false, and not to be accepted?

_____ 22. Are you presenting any of the evidence from the various fields of science which help establish the creation model as a superior model of origins?

_____ 23. Are you presenting material in your classes **against** the creation model of origins?

_____ 24. Are you using in your classes materials written by humanists and/or evolutionists (e.g., books like *Science and Creationism* by Dr. Ashley Montagu, *Abusing Science: The Case Against Creationism* by Dr. Philip Kitcher, etc.)?

_____ 25. If your answer to question #24 above is 'yes,' are you using these materials in order to **refute**

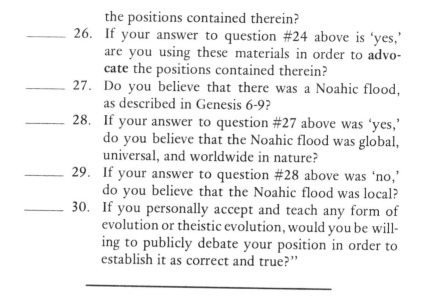

the positions contained therein?

_____ 26. If your answer to question #24 above is 'yes,' are you using these materials in order to **advocate** the positions contained therein?

_____ 27. Do you believe that there was a Noahic flood, as described in Genesis 6-9?

_____ 28. If your answer to question #27 above was 'yes,' do you believe that the Noahic flood was global, universal, and worldwide in nature?

_____ 29. If your answer to question #28 above was 'no,' do you believe that the Noahic flood was local?

_____ 30. If you personally accept and teach any form of evolution or theistic evolution, would you be willing to publicly debate your position in order to establish it as correct and true?"

"Dear Dr. Williams:

[For text of first eight paragraphs of this letter, refer to previous letter to Archie Manis. The text in both letters is identical.]

"One or two examples will certainly suffice. One of the overhead transparencies which you have been using in class is entitled, 'Phylogenetic History.' That particular transparency discusses, for example, 'the invasion of land by an undifferentiated thalloid plant (not later than Silurian, perhaps as early as Cambrian),. . .the evolution of the pollen algae,. . .evolution of the bisporangiate flower (Triassic),. . .evolution of the herbaceous habit (Cretaceous, but chiefly Cenozoic),' etc. Upon seeing this material in printed form, I asked the student(s) who sent it if the material on it was **refuted**. They said it was **not** refuted, but was instead taught as **factual**! In addition, one student wrote to explain that so **much** evolution-oriented material was presented on the **first day of class** that he immediately withdrew from the class. His friends who remained in the class later spoke with him regarding how much more **additional evolution-oriented** material had been used, almost on a daily basis! Further, one of the professors in the biology department is using as his class text the book, *Science and Creationism*, edited by Dr. Ashley Montagu. I know all too well of Dr. Montagu, and this particular book. Dr. Montagu is the renowned humanist/evolutionist who recently went on record as stating that 'absolute truth belongs only to one class of humans. . .the class of absolute fools' (*The Atlanta Journal and Constitution*, 7-26-81, p 4-C). Dr. Montagu's aversion to the Bible, God, and related matters is too well-documented to need comment. And anyone even vaguely familiar with evolution and its adherents in humanism today would recognize the 'who's who' of humanistic/evolutionary thought that were contributors to the book which Dr. Montagu edited (and which one professor is using in his attempts to present evolution and refute creationism). The names of men like Isaac Asimov, Stephen Jay Gould, Gunther Stent, and Garrett Hardin are well-known to those of us who are constantly in the battle against humanism and its system of evolutionary origins. Upon receiving a large packet of materials to document the students' claims, and upon seeing the photocopy of the frontispiece from the Montagu book, I picked up the phone (again, to give the professor the benefit of the doubt) and telephoned one of the students to ask if it was possible that the professor was simply using the book as an 'example' of evolutionary thought, in order to refute the claims made in the book. This particular student said that it was quite the reverse—the claims of the book against creationism, and the God behind creation, were being vindicated in class. The student said that in order to convince me, copies of the handouts used in class could be sent. They **were** sent, and I have them sitting here in my office as I write you this letter. I am amazed and appalled at what I see. One of the handouts, authored by an ACU professor, is entitled, 'Research in Genesis.' Attached to it is a photocopy of the first page of the Bible, containing Genesis 1. Out beside the biblical text, in the margin, are the professor's markings to the students. When I read out beside Genesis 1:1 the comment that it was a 'hymn' or 'creation myth,' I was left speechless. How a professor in a **Christian** college or university, much less my own alma mater, could advocate such was beyond my comprehension.

"The documentation which I have received certainly

speaks for itself. I have never seen such a motley assortment of anti-creationist materials in a Christian college environment before. From photocopied handouts (given to the students) of material from Philip Kitcher's recent book, *Abusing Science: The Case Against Creationism*, to one professor's own 'Evolution Notes,' these materials represent some of the most venemous materials I have ever come across. For me to be presented with the fact that such materials are being used at my own alma mater, to undermine the faith of precious young minds, causes me a grief which I cannot adequately express to you in this letter!

"Dr. Williams, the purpose of this letter is two-fold. First, I am writing you to ask an explanation of these ongoings. As an alumnus of the University, as a former student in the very department where these things are being taught, and as a brother in the Lord, I feel I have every right to inquire regarding these matters. I do not have to tell you by now that I am **very** disturbed at the documentation I have seen. The students' charges have been proven true by the very information which has been presented in class. There is no doubt that an explanation from you is in order. I, personally, would appreciate one. No doubt, others would as well, Second, I am writing to provide you an opportunity to respond to these allegations. If I have 'misunderstood,' then this letter is my request that you help me to properly understand. If you feel that some of the documentation was inappropriate, then this letter will provide you with an opportunity to correct that as well.

"In an attempt to better understand exactly what you **do** believe regarding these matters, and to properly and correctly understand what you **are** teaching, I am asking you to please provide me with answers to the questions which you will find listed below. These are questions which any Christian ought to be able to answer quickly and easily, as they represent 'basics' among us. They are intended to elicit simply a 'yes' or 'no' answer; however, should you feel that more is needed, please do not hesitate to append whatever response you feel is justified.

"I will eagerly await your response, as I am anxious to see a solution to this problem, which is affecting the faith of young people under your tutelage, and at **my** alma mater. I deem this to be a problem of no little significance, and I wish you to know that I would like to do anything humanly possible to ensure that the situation as it now stands does not continue.

Sincerely,
(signed) Bert Thompson, Ph.D.
Professor of Bible & Science
Alabama Christian School of Religion

"Attachment

[The questions that were attached to this letter are identical to the ones attached to the previous letter to Dr. Manis, except for question #24, which is reproduced below.]

_____ 24. Are you using in your classes materials (books, portions of books, articles, etc.) written by humanists and/or evolutionists?"

Our correspondence to Drs. Manis and Williams was dated, and mailed, March 27, 1985. On April 3, 1985 we received **one** of the certified mail return receipts, signed by Kenneth Williams, indicating that he had received our letter. However, the return receipt never came from Archie Manis' letter. On April 11, 1985, the **original letter**, which we had mailed to Dr. Manis, came back to us marked, "REFUSED." At the time we received the letter, we surmised that possibly the following turn of events had taken place: Since both letters were mailed on the same day from Montgomery, Alabama, by certified mail, likely both would have arrived at the ACU Post Office on the same day. Apparently Dr. Williams went to the campus Post Office, received (and signed for) his letter, opened it, noted the contents, and "warned" Manis regarding the same. Dr. Manis, then, upon being asked to sign for the letter, chose instead to refuse it. It subsequently was returned to us unopened and unread. [NOTE: We later discovered, in a meeting which took place with ACU officials on September 13, 1985, that this is **exactly** what happened.] Upon the return of Dr. Manis' "refused" certified letter, we then sent the professor (by regular mail) a postcard, stating that his refusal of our letter by no means absolved him of the responsibility of its contents, and that he had two additional weeks to respond to the items set forth in the Williams letter (to which he was obviously privy).

We heard nothing from either professor. Had it not been for the fact that we sent the original letters by certified mail with return receipts, we would not have known that Dr. Williams received his letter. As we were preparing then to carry our inquiries up the "chain of command" at the University (Department Head, Dean, President, Board), a letter from Dr. Perry Reeves, Dean of the College of Natural and Applied Sciences, arrived in our office on April 16, 1985. Dr. Reeves' letter was dated April 12, 1985 and is photographically reproduced below.

[See page 35 for photoreproduction of Dr. Reeves' letter.]

ABILENE CHRISTIAN UNIVERSITY

915/677-1911 Abilene, Texas 79699

April 12, 1985

Dr. Bert Thompson
230 Landmark Drive
Montgomery, Alabama 36117-2752

Dear Dr. Thompson:

Dr. Ken Williams has shared with me your letter of March 27, 1985 and I
appreciate your interest in Abilene Christian University. Earlier this
semester I had talked to Mark Scott and was aware of his deep concerns.
After he came to me, I talked to Dr. Williams, Dr. Manis, the Department
Chairman and several other students in the classes under question.

I know Dr. Williams and Dr. Manis and I know of their belief in and love
for God. They are dedicated men — dedicated to the Church and to the
University and its students. Dr. Manis is an elder in a local congregation and preaches many times each year. It is their intent to expose
our students to the way in which evolutionists think and to expose them
to evolutionists' claims so that these students will be better equipped
to face attacks on their faith when they leave ACU and enter professional/
graduate schools or the business world. In no way is it our intent to
destroy or cripple the faith of our students.

We believe that God is the Creator and Sustainer of the Universe. Our
purpose is to educate students so that they might glorify Him in their
daily lives and might be servants to their fellowman as was His Son.
Pray for us as we attempt to fulfill this mission.

Sincerely,

Perry C. Reeves, Dean
College of Natural and Applied Sciences

nc

As the reader examines the letter, the following points will surely be of interest. First, we had not written to Dr. Reeves. We had written specifically (and privately) to Drs. Manis and Williams. Second, even one of those men (Dr. Manis) **refused** our original letter. Third, notice that Dr. Reeves' letter specifically mentions Mark Scott by name, even though at this point in time University officials did not know that Mark Scott had been the one to initially contact us (we had specifically omitted his name from any of our correspondence for fear that he might suffer reprisals at the hands of the two professors—a fear that later proved to be well-founded). Notice, too, that Dr. Reeves' letter mentions that he had, even at this early point in the controversy, already spoken with Mark Scott and "several other students." It is clear from the content of Dr. Reeves' letter that the scope and magnitude of the problem, even early on, was significant enough to warrant intervention by the Dean of the College. In other words, it had already progressed from the Department Head level to the office of the Dean! [We would find out weeks later, in fact, that it had already gone far beyond that—all the way through the Vice-President for Academic Affairs to the Board of Trustees of the University.] Fourth, notice what is conspicuously missing from Dr. Reeves' letter: (A) any response(s) to the questions which had been appended to the Manis and Williams letters; (B) the reason(s) for Dr. Manis' refusal of our original letter to him; (C) any explanation concerning the use of evolution-oriented textbooks written by humanists in ACU biology classes; (D) an explanation of the use of handouts belittling the creation account as per Genesis 1 and denigrating the Bible in general; (E) an explanation of Dr. Manis' statement that evolution is a "fact"; (F) an explanation of how an ACU biology professor could write "myth" across the Genesis account of creation; (G) an explanation as to why students would write, complaining that these two professors were out-and-out theisitc evolutionists. Further, notice the "general" statement in the last paragraph of Dr. Reeves' letter that "We believe that God is the Creator and Sustainer of the Universe," and the complete avoidance of any specifics regarding theistic evolution, the literal, historical nature of the Genesis account of creation, etc.—

all of which were items emphasized in our original letters to the two professors.

Dr. Reeves' letter did not provide answers to **any** of the questions which we had raised in our appeal to Drs. Manis and Williams, and we feel was quite obviously an attempt to "paper over" the serious nature of the issues involved. On April 29, 1985 we penned a letter to Dr. Reeves, stressing several major points. First, we made it clear that our letter to him was not to be considered an "official response" in any way. We had written the two professors, and were waiting for the allotted time period (which we had offered for them to respond) to pass. Then, in keeping with our previously published agenda, we would continue following the chain of command through proper channels. Second, we pointed out that we were surprised to be receiving a letter from the Dean, since **we had not even written the Dean**. Third, we made certain that Dean Reeves understood that his letter (which was only three short paragraphs) did not even begin to address the issues involved. Fourth, we noted that we were curious as to why the professors could not answer for themselves, since our inquiries concerned **their** teachings, and since they were, after all, Ph.D.'s— quite capable of writing a single letter or answering a few questions. In short, we made it clear to Dean Reeves that his letter was not satisfactory, and that we fully intended to have answers to the questions which we had raised. The letter which we wrote Dr. Reeves is reproduced below. [Note that along with our letter to Dr. Reeves we enclosed our **original** letter to Dr. Manis, so that Dean Reeves could hand-carry it to him for any response he might wish to make.]

"Dear Dean Reeves:

"I have recently been in both Texas and Oklahoma, delivering various lectures on creation/evolution, and have just returned to find your letter of April 12 on my desk. I apologize for the delay in responding, but I have been out of town for almost two weeks, and this accounts for the delayed response.

"I appreciate you taking the time and effort to write, but

I must admit that I am somewhat surprised to be receiving a letter from you. As you know, I wrote Drs. Kenneth Williams and Archie Manis **personal** letters, and did not send you, or the biology department head, or any other administrative personnel, copies of those letters. There was, of course, a reason for that. From the very beginning of this controversy, when several students from ACU contacted our offices requesting assistance because they were having 'evolution crammed down their throats' (to use their words), we have been very careful to handle this matter in a most professional, and Christian, manner. Only after weeks of in-depth study into the matter did we then write the two professors. And we have been very careful **not** to 'go behind their backs' in any way, by writing their department head, academic dean, etc. We wrote each of them **personally**, in order to give them an appropriate opportunity to admit or deny the charges against them (and I think it certainly goes without saying that the charges are of a most serious nature!).

"For that reason, I am surprised to be receiving a letter from the Dean. We have not even received any response from the professors yet. And that being the case, your letter is even more surprising! Let me, for purposes of clarification, re-state what we intend to do.

"We mailed personal letters, by certified mail with return receipt, to both Drs. Manis and Williams. We have the return receipt, signed by Dr. Williams, indicating that he did receive his letter. As you may or may not know, Dr. Manis refused his letter, obviously hoping to avoid these issues. We then sent Dr. Manis a postcard, acknowledging his refusal of our letter, and putting him on notice that unless he corresponded with us within two weeks from the date on the postcard, we would begin making public our inquiry into this matter.

"When the two week date passes, that will have given Dr. Williams, who **did** receive our letter, over a month to have been able to respond to the letter, and our pledge to Dr. Manis will have been kept. Once that time frame has been completed, it is then our intention to write to the Department Head, Dr. Little, sending him copies of our letters, and asking for a written response from him to these matters. We intend to give him an adequate time in which to respond. If no response is forthcoming from Dr. Little, we will then write you for your response, which of course will have to explain how it is that a Christian University, supported in large part by funds from members of the churches of Christ, can allow the destructive teaching of organic evolution to occur, **and continue**, in its science department. If no adequate explanation is forthcoming from your office, we fully intend then to write to President Teague. If an adequate response is not forthcoming from his office, we then intend to write the Board of Directors. If they are unable to assist us in finding a way to stop the teaching of the atheistic system of evolution by Drs. Manis and Williams, we will then have no choice but to publish for widespread distribution the results of our attempts, through **proper administrative channels**, to halt the teaching at ACU of atheistic or theistic evolution in the biology department.

"We have 'gone the extra mile' in this matter, making certain that our actions followed proper procedure and took advantage of proper administrative routes. We did **not** send copies of our personal letters to Drs. Manis and Williams to any other administrative personnel. In addition, our letters offered an opportunity to these two professors to either acknowledge or deny the charges levelled against them, and to explain themselves in full. Apparently the questions appended to our letters were a bit too explicit for either of the professors to answer without putting themselves into quite a predicament, due to the fact of having to admit, via the answers to the questions, to teaching atheistic or theistic evolution to the students. In any case, we fully intend to follow our initial agenda, so that should this matter not be resolved to our satisfaction (viz., Drs. Manis and Williams stop teaching atheistic and/or theistic evolution to students under their tutelage), when the material is made public, brethren will see that we acted as Christians, and made every possible attempt to allow the matter to be corrected.

"For the above-mentioned reasons, this letter to you is not to be construed in any way as an official response to your letter of April 12. It is merely an acknowledgment of the receipt of your letter, and our way of letting you know the agenda which we are following. Once the proper time frame for a response (with answers to our questions) from Drs.

Williams and Manis has passed, Dr. Little may then expect a letter from us, with appropriate questions as well. Upon a response (or lack of) from him, we will then be in touch with you by personal letter in order to further attempt a solution to this unfortunate entanglement in error by two professors under your direction. It is our hope, of course, that those involved will repent, make restitution, and not commit the same mistake again in the future.

"In closing, may I make one more comment. You stated in your letter, in speaking of these two professors in the biology department, that 'it is their intent to expose our students to the way in which evolutionists think and to expose them to evolutionists' claims so that these students will be better equipped to face attacks on their faith when they leave ACU and enter professional/graduate schools or the business world.' May I kindly suggest, Dean Reeves, that you must not be privy to what your two professors are teaching. Consider, for example, the materials handed out by Dr. Manis in his classes, and **authored by him**, entitled 'Evolution Notes' (five pages). On page three, under #14, Dr. Manis states very specifically that 'Evolution's history and methodology will continue to feed debates for generations, but the **fact** of evolution is **beyond dispute**. The concept is **rational, scientific**, and supported by an **overwhelming mass of evidence** from past and present.'

"Now honestly, Dean Reeves, does that sound to **you** like Dr. Manis is teaching the students how to **reject** evolution and thereby save their precious faith? If so, I for one would like an explanation as to why professors are advocating **rejection** of that which is 'rational, scientific, and supported by an overwhelming mass of evidence from past and present'! I think other brethren around the country would like the same question answered. One way or another, we intend to see to it that the question **is** answered.

"We will be back in touch with you upon receiving a response from Drs. Williams and Manis, or after having allowed an adequate time for such a response to be sent, even though it has not been. In the meantime, my suggestion to you, with due respect for your position and title of course, is that you get ahold of some of the same materials that have been sent to us (class handouts, class textbooks, class transparencies, class tests, etc.) and examine them more closely before you defend, in print, the professors whom you say are **not** 'destroying or crippling' the faith of ACU students. I think you will be shocked at what you find, and that the evidence indicates exactly the opposite.

Respectfully,
(signed) Bert Thompson, Ph.D.

"Enclosure(s)

"PS: Dr. Manis refused our certified letter. Since you have written to us regarding these matters, and since you are obviously now involved, I am taking the liberty of sending you the **original** letter sent to Dr. Manis. I think you will want to read it. And may I request that you handcarry it to Dr. Manis? I think he'll want to read it, now that he knows the agenda we intend to follow."

———————————

We continued to wait for a response from the two professors. In fact, we waited until May 16, 1985 (remember: our first letter to the professors was sent on March 27, 1985). Approximately two months had now passed, and still no response of any kind had been received from Manis and Williams. At this time, in keeping with what we had told Dr. Reeves we would do, we then mailed a letter to Dr. John Little, Chairman of the biology department at ACU, and the man who is ultimately responsible for what Drs. Manis and Williams teach in his department. Dr. Little was, of course, next in the University's "chain of command" and so it was to him that we wrote, asking for an explanation of these ongoings. It came as no great surprise when Dr. Little did not respond to our letter. It was apparent by this time that a "cover-up" of significant proportions was beginning to take shape. Little did we know just **how** significant the proportions were. As unbelievable as it may sound, we would later discover, in a meeting with ACU officials, that those at the University—from the two professors all the way up to the President—had been ordered **by the Board of Trustees**—to completely ignore our letters! Below is a copy of our May 16th letter to Dr. Little.

"Dear Dr. Little:

"Greetings from those of us associated with the work of Apologetics Press, Inc.

"Several months ago we received telephone calls and letters from certain students at Abilene Christian University requesting assistance in dealing with a very serious problem on campus. It seems that these students were, to use their very words, 'having evolution crammed down' their throats by certain professors in the biology department. Our work here at Apologetics Press, Inc. is fairly well-known, and our materials are quite wide-spread. Some of the students had seen some of our materials, and called or wrote to inquire about securing additional materials and advice on how to deal with the problem of being taught evolution at Abilene Christian University. [NOTE: At the outset, let me make the definitions of my terms clear to you. When I employ the word 'evolution' I am discussing the General Theory of Evolution, i.e., organic evolution, as the term is generally employed in the scientific community.]

"Naturally, being an alumnus of both the University and the biology department, I was at first incredulous to these claims. However, after weeks and weeks of intensive investigation, which included an in-depth examination of handout materials, overhead transparencies, classroom textbooks, and other materials currently being used by certain professors in the biology department, it became quite apparent that the charges levelled by the students were fully substantiated, and warranted our immediate attention.

"Subsequently, I penned a **personal** letter to the two professors involved, Dr. Kenneth Williams and Dr. Archie Manis. My letters to these two men were self-explanatory; no doubt you have already seen copies of them, since I understand (via a recent letter from your Dean) that copies have been widely circulated. I did **not** send copies of my letters to these two professors to any other administrative personnel, and that was purposely done for several reasons. First, I wanted to present the professors involved with an opportunity to deny, or explain, the charges before anyone else became involved. Second, I wanted to act in a Christian manner and, as a brother in Christ, approach these two gentlemen privately so that hopefully this situation could be corrected privately. Third, I did not want to be accused of 'going behind their backs' by writing to their department head, dean, etc. either before, or at the same time as, I was writing to them.

"My letters to Drs. Williams and Manis were mailed on March 27, 1985. They were sent by certified mail with return receipt, so that we would know that each man did, in fact, receive his letter. Several days later, the certified postal receipt from Dr. Williams' letter arrived in our offices, signed by him and thereby indicating he had received our correspondence. A day or so later, Dr. Manis' entire letter was returned to us, marked 'REFUSED.' Apparently Dr. Williams received his letter first at the ACU post office, read it, alerted Dr. Manis to its content (even though their two letters were not identical) and Dr. Manis therefore chose to refuse our letter. At that time we then sent Dr. Manis a postcard by routine mail delivery, acknowledging his refusal of our letter, and putting him on notice that unless he reconsidered and responded to our inquiry, we would proceed to make this matter public in nature, rather than private.

"Shortly afterwards, I received a one-page letter (dated April 12, 1985) from your Dean, Dr. Perry Reeves, attempting both to placate us and to convince us that these two professors, despite the available evidence, were not teaching evolution in the classrooms at ACU, except possibly to refute it. I wrote Dr. Reeves on April 29, 1985 to acknowledge his letter, but making it clear that my letter to him was **not** a response of any kind. I made it clear in my letter that we were waiting, as we said we would, for a two-week period from the date of my postcard to Dr. Manis, so that Drs. Williams and Manis would have ample time to respond to our letters. I also made it clear to Dean Reeves that apparently he had not investigated the matter as fully as he should, else he would not be defending two biology professors who **most certainly are** teaching evolution—and to **advocate** it, not refute it. I quoted to Dr. Reeves the statement from the classroom handouts authored by Dr. Manis himself ('Evolution Notes'—five pages) where he specifically states: 'Evolution's history and methodology will continue to feed debates for generations, but the **fact** of evolution is **beyond dispute**. The concept is **rational, scientific,** and supported by an **overwhelming mass of evidence** from past and present' (page 3, under number 14). As I stated to Dr. Reeves in my letter to him, there can be little doubt, after reading a statement as clearly written as that, where Dr. Manis stands, and what 'kind' of evolution he is teaching students at Abilene Christian University.

"The additional two weeks which we allowed Drs. Manis and Williams to use in responding to our March 27th letter have now passed. We have therefore allowed them well over a month (all of April and half of May) in which to formulate a response and answer the questions which we appended to our letter(s). Now, in keeping with the agenda which we told Dr. Reeves we would follow, we are writing you, their department head, for an explanation of these matters.

"Dr. Little, there can be absolutely no doubt that these two men are teaching atheistic and/or theistic evolution to students under their tutelage. And there can be no doubt that their refusal to respond to our letters, and to answer our questions, is clear indication that they do not wish to have it made public what they are, in fact, teaching. In fact, Dr. Manis' refusal to even accept our letter tells far more than he intended it to! In any case, the problem of the teaching of the godless, atheistic, humanistic system of evolution at a **Christian** university, whose programs are supported in large part by contributions from members of the churches of Christ, cannot be ignored. I, for one, do not intend to ignore it, or to allow such teaching(s) to go unchecked.

"The evidence that Drs. Manis and Williams, two professors under your immediate direction, **are** teaching atheistic and/or theistic evolution is indisputable, and we are prepared to make that evidence public should the need arise. However, in keeping with our planned (and published—see the copy of our letter to Dean Reeves) agenda, we are now writing you to ask you for an explanation to these matters, and to ask you to aid us in seeing to it that these false teachings do not occur and that the men responsible for them repent and do not continue in such error.

"Attached to this letter is a listing of several questions which we are asking you to answer. Drs. Manis and Williams have so far adamantly refused to answer our questions. We certainly hope that you will not follow suit, since a refusal would, as it has in the case of Williams and Manis, indicate that you (and they) have something to hide. The appended questions may ultimately be divided into two groups. The first group represents questions which any Christian ought to be able to answer quickly and easily, as they represent 'basics' among us. The second group represents questions which deal specifically with the teaching of evolution at ACU. Each question is intended to elicit a simple 'yes' or 'no' answer; however, should you feel that more is needed, please do not hesitate to append whatever response you feel is justified. We will eagerly await your response, as we are anxious to see a solution to this problem, which is adversely affecting the faith of young people studying with professors under your direction, and at a **Christian** university. We deem this problem to be of significant magnitude, and I wish you to know that we do not intend to sit quietly by while compromising professors attack the faith of precious young minds.

Sincerely,
(signed) Bert Thompson, Ph. D.
Professor of Bible & Science
Alabama Christian School of Religion

"Attachment

"PS: Now that a more-than-ample time span has been allowed for Drs. Manis and Williams to respond to our March 27th letter; now that they have refused to make any response; now that our letter(s) are beginning to flow through proper adminsitrative channels; and, now that upper-level administrators (e.g., Dean Reeves) are actively involved in the situation as it now stands, we will begin sending copies of this correspondence **both** to ACU administrators, **and to other interested parties**, as per our promise to Dr. Manis in our earlier postcard to him. We truly regret that this has become necessary, but then it could have been avoided had Drs. Manis and Williams answered our original letters.

PPS: Questions 26ff will be of special interest to you as Department Head.

[Questions 1-18 are exactly the same as questions 1-18 in the Manis and Williams letters. Questions 19-40 are new and/or different and are reproduced below.]

_____ 19. Do you believe that there was a Noahic flood as described in Genesis 6-9?

_____ 20. If your answer to question #19 above was 'yes,' do you believe that the Noahic flood was global, universal, and worldwide in nature?

_____ 21. If your answer to question #20 above was 'no,' do you believe that the Noahic flood was local in nature?

_____ 22. Do you teach theistic evolution (i.e., that the theory of evolution as taught in most scientific circles today may be accepted at the same time as belief in God) in your classes at Abilene Christian University?

_____ 23. Are you refuting the General Theory of Evolution (i.e., organic evolution) in your classes, in an attempt to make certain that your students understand it is false, and not to be accepted?

_____ 24. Are you presenting any of the evidence from the various fields of science which help to establish the creation model as the superior model of origins?

_____ 25. Are you presenting material in your classes **against** the creation model of origins?

_____ 26. To your knowledge, are any of the professors under your immediate direction in the Department of Biology at Abilene Christian University publicly teaching in their classes (and advocating that their students accept as a factual, correct account for the origin of the universe and life forms in that universe) either organic evolution or theistic evolution?

_____ 27. If it could be proven to you that certain professors under your direction, and in the Biology Department for which you serve as Chairman, **are** teaching and advocating the acceptance of either organic evolution or theistic evolution, would you take appropriate administrative steps to see to it that these men were reprimanded, repented and did not continue such teachings?

_____ 28. If it could be proven to you that certain professors under your direction, and in the Biology Department for which you serve as Chairman, **are** teaching and advocating the acceptance of either organic evolution or theistic evolution, would you allow such teaching to continue?

_____ 29. One of the professors under your direction, Dr. Archie Manis, has been using as a textbook for one of the courses he teaches the blatantly anti-creationist book, _Science and Creationism_, edited by the famous evolutionist/humanist, Dr. Ashley Montagu. Were you aware, prior to the beginnings of our correspondence with professors at ACU, of Dr. Manis' use of this textbook in his biology classes?

_____ 30. If your answer to question #29 above is 'yes,' were you aware of the fact that the Montagu book openly attacks the biblical doctrines of creation, God, etc.?

_____ 31. If your answer to question #30 above was 'yes,' did you approve the use of the book anway?

_____ 32. If your answer to question #29 above was 'no,' and you were not aware of the use of the Montagu textbook in an ACU biology class, once you **were** made aware of the use of such a book (e.g., through our correspondence) did you then initiate steps to see to it that the book was either removed from the classroom, or that the anti-creation, anti-God concepts which the book presents were openly **refuted** in the classroom?

_____ 33. Is it true that at the end of the spring semester in 1985 you, or certain professors in the Department of Biology at Abilene Christian University, handed out a teacher-evaluation form to certain (or all) classes which had to be signed by the students completing it, and which contained the following statements: 'As you are undoubtedly aware, the subject of evolution can be a sensitive issue in a Christian college context. In view of the fact that the subject has been an integral part of this course, we would appreciate your opinions as they relate to the presentation of the material in this class. The professor will not have access to your response until after grades have been turned in.'?

_____ 34. **Has** evolution been taught 'as an integral part' of biology classes at Abilene Christian University, as the teacher-evaluation form mentioned in question #33 above so states?

_____ 35. Has it been standard procedure at Abilene Christian University in the past to **require** that students **sign** their teacher-evaluation forms?

_____ 36. If the answer to question #35 above is 'no,' was the requirement that students in certain biology classes **sign** their teacher-evaluation forms an attempt on the part of certain professors or certain administrators to 'identify' certain students who have publicly or privately opposed the teaching of evolution on the campus at Abilene Christian University?

_____ 37. To your knowledge, have any students (i.e., one or more) made attempts to discuss the teaching of evolution or theistic evolution as factual in the Department of Biology at Abilene Christian University with you or any other administrator?

_____ 38. Are you, as Chairman of the Department of Biology, aware of the fact that Dr. Archie Manis has been handing out in his classes reprints from anti-creationist literature (e.g., chapters from Dr. Philip Kitcher's book, *Abusing Science: The Case Against Creationism*) and urging the students to accept as correct the positions against creationism as advocated by such anti-creationist authors?

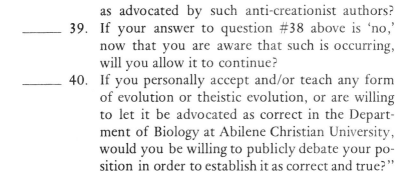

_____ 39. If your answer to question #38 above is 'no,' now that you are aware that such is occurring, will you allow it to continue?

_____ 40. If you personally accept and/or teach any form of evolution or theistic evolution, or are willing to let it be advocated as correct in the Department of Biology at Abilene Christian University, would you be willing to publicly debate your position in order to establish it as correct and true?''

In the meantime, however, other facts began to come to light. For example, on June 3, 1985 we received another letter from Mark Scott. Mark had just received his grades for the spring semester. To his surprise, he discovered that his grades in two of his biology classes (one class under Dr. Manis, one class under Dr. Williams) had been **lowered** by a minimum of one letter grade! In Dr. Manis' biology seminar class, Mark had earned (according to his papers and class participation) an "A" or a "B"—but was given a "C". When he went, personally, to Dr. Manis to inquire as to why his grade had been lowered, Dr. Manis lost no time in telling him (as recorded in Scott's June 1 letter): "the real reason I got a 'C' was because it was the only way he could get rid of his anger and keep him from taking me, you, and your 'outfit' to court and suing us." Dr. Manis quickly went on to tell Mark Scott that his grade had been lowered because Mark did not agree with the evolution that Dr. Manis had taught in class. Mark Scott's letter, relating these happenings, is reproduced below.

"Dear Dr. Thompson:

"I received my grades for the spring semester at Abilene yesterday, and was surprised to see a couple of undeserved grades from 2 of my biology courses. I was given a 'C' in Seminar in Biology when I earned an 'A' or a 'B' and in Botany Lab I received a 'D' when I deserved an 'A' or 'B'. These 2 grades kept me from getting on the Dean's List.

"I asked Manis yesterday why I received a 'C' when we were told the quizzes in the class would be used to separate the 'A's' from the 'B's.' At first he said he felt I didn't grasp the subject well enough. I asked him on what basis he felt that, since the quizzes indicated I did well in the class. Then he said that I was the only one in the class who had declared open warfare against him and the school and had got help from someone in Alabama and said that for that reason he had photocopied my quizzes. I told him that what he meant to say was that I got a 'C' in the class because I didn't agree with what he taught. He then got upset and said that the real reason I got a 'C' was because it was the only way he could get rid of his anger and keep him from taking me, you, and your 'outfit' to court and suing us. But he said he wanted to be a Christian about it. I then stopped him and asked him on what basis he could sue us, and he got **real** upset and said he didn't ever want to talk to me again, showed me to the door and told me he didn't want me taking any more of his classes. He said all that. I told him I would be taking more of his classes and left, and then presented my case to Dr. Little and Dr. Reeves and told them what Manis had said, and showed them my quiz grades which they photocopied and said they would talk to Manis. Unfortunately, the Academic Board does not meet over the summer and my lab teacher and Williams are gone to Mexico right now. I don't remember if I told you in my last letter, but I received an unbelievable 21 out of 100 points on my lab notebook, when I had put a lot of work into my labs and conscienciously kept up with my projects and a friend of mine who had become a friend of Williams received a 100. When I had asked for my notebook back earlier, Williams said I would have to wait until he photocopied it; but all my other grades in the class were real good.

"Dr. Little said that I have to understand that Manis has been going through a lot lately, and that since Bert Thompson has been 'poking around,' nobody in the school has been acting normally. I told him that was no excuse to make more mistakes. I suggested to Dr. Little that he might want to remind Manis what the Bible says in Mt. 18 how I am to handle someone who sins against me.

"I don't need to tell you how surprised I am that they

would resort to tampering with my grades, especially after such things as trying to throw me out of class because of my creation views. This is a very serious matter. I hate to say this,. . .but it appears your predictions of things getting hot around here were correct, the more I find out what is really going on inside A.C.U.

(signed) Mark"

In addition to his grade being lowered in the biology seminar class, Mark also had a grade lowered in his Botany Lab (for which Dr. Kenneth Williams is responsible). The grade assigned to Mark was a "D". During the fall semester, 1985, Mark appealed the lowering of his lab grade to the Academic Council of the College of Natural and Applied Sciences. [NOTE: The appeal was made during the fall of 1985 because the Academic Council does not meet during summer sessions.] Interestingly, the Chairman of the Council is none other than Dr. Perry Reeves, Dean of the College of Natural and Applied Sciences. There are **no students** on the Academic Council. Mark's appeal was subsequently denied. As this publication goes to press, Mark is appealing through the office of the Vice-President for Academic Affairs to the **University** Academic Council, in order to ask that his Botany Lab grade be changed. [NOTE: The grade in Dr. Manis' seminar class was later changed **back** to the "B" it should have been in the first place. The reason for that change will be discussed at-length in the pages which follow. The events which necessitated the grade change **are interesting indeed.**]

Let us at this point interject an observation. Later in this document, the reader will observe that ACU officials have charged that "no students have ever come forth in the past" to complain about the teaching of evolution in these biology classes. The petty lament has also been offered that "it is certainly odd that no students ever speak up against the teaching of evolution in our classes." We will deal with such statements in full at a later point in this publication. But let us at least remark right here that, considering the treatment given a student who **did** speak up, it is a little difficult to take the statements of ACU officials seriously when they "wonder" why no student comes forward to "speak up." The students know full-well that the same thing that happened to Mark Scott might just happen to them! And besides, we will shortly show the statement to be **false** which contends that "no students have ever come forth in the past" to complain about the teaching of evolution. In fact, both students and students' parents **have** "come forth" in the past to complain about the teaching of evolution in the biology department, and we have the documentation to prove it! What we are seeing here on the part of ACU officials is this: a panicky cover-up as a last-ditch effort to keep inquiring brethren from discovering the real truth as to what is now going on, and what has been going on, for a long, long time at ACU.

Our letter to Dr. Little, dated May 16, 1985, went completely ignored, as had our letters to Manis and Williams. However, in keeping with our pledge to follow the appropriate University channels, we then wrote, on August 12, 1985 (having allowed almost three months for Dr. Little to answer our letter) Dr. Perry Reeves, Dean of the College of Natural and Applied Sciences. Our letter to Dr. Reeves is reproduced below.

"Dear Dr. Reeves:

[For text of first four paragraphs of this letter, refer to previous letter to Dr. Little. The text in both letters is identical.]

"My letters to Drs. Manis and Williams were mailed on March 27, 1985 by certified mail with return receipt so that we would know that each man did, in fact, receive his letter. As you are now no doubt aware, Dr. Williams accepted his letter, while Dr. Manis refused his. To date, neither man has answered, or responded to in any way, our letter(s).

"That being the case, I then penned a letter to their Department Head, Dr. John Little. My letter to Dr. Little was dated May 16, 1985. In that letter, I asked Dr. Little to please confirm, or deny (with appropriate evidence) the charges made against the faculty members who serve under his direction. To date (and it has been almost three months!) we have received no reply from Dr. Little.

-52-

"Since both the professors involved, and their Department Head, have adamantly refused to even respond to our letters, we are now writing you, the Dean of the College of Natural and Applied Sciences at Abilene Christian University. As we have stated in previous letters, it is our full intent to carry this matter in a correct manner through proper administrative channels, all the way to the Board of Directors if need be. Since neither the professors nor their Department Head has had the Christian demeanor or common decency to acknowledge, or respond to, our letters, you, as the Dean, are now next in line for us to contact.

"Dr. Reeves, there can be absolutely **no doubt** that these two men are teaching atheistic and/or theistic evolution to students under their tutelage. And there can be no doubt that their refusal to respond to our letters, and to answer our questions, is clear indication that they do not wish to have it made public what they are, in fact, teaching. Further, their own actions since our first letter have substantiated the charges against them. For example, at the end of the spring semester, a questionnaire/teacher-evaluation sheet was handed out to students in certain biology classes. One of the questions on that questionnaire read as follows: 'As you are undoubtedly aware, the subject of evolution can be a sensitive issue in a Christian college context. In view of the fact that the subject has been an integral part of this course, we would appreciate your opinions as they relate to the presentation of the material in class. The professor will not have access to your response until after grades have been turned in.'

"Now, Dr. Reeves, **has** the teaching of evolution been 'an integral part' of the biology courses at Abilene Christian University? All along you, and others directly involved in this controversy, have been telling both students and those from outside the University community that 'We are **not** teaching evolution in biology classes at Abilene Christian University!' Yet the very questionnaire which you forced the students to complete plainly admits to the teaching of evolution as an 'integral part' of the classes. With all due respect, Dr. Reeves, I should think that you would want to get together with the parties involved and at least get your stories straight! It appears that the right hand doesn't know what the left hand is doing.

"There are now several other matters that must likewise be cleared up. First of course, you, as Dean, are going to have to answer this question: Why did Dr. Manis (whom you described in an April 12, 1985 letter as a 'dedicated man' and 'elder who preaches many times each year') act in so unChristian a manner as to actually give one of the students in his seminar class a **lower** grade than he actually deserved, just because that particular student publicly, in class, took issue with Dr. Manis' teaching of organic evolution and ridiculing of the Genesis account of creation? Is it standard policy for your 'dedicated' teachers (and men who are at least by name elders in the Lord's church) to illegally tamper with student grades and actually give a student a grade lower than he or she should have received?

"Second, why is Dr. Manis **still** being allowed to teach evolution in his classes this summer, even as this letter is being penned to you? Only a day or so ago we received yet another telephone call, documenting—from a student who is now taking general biology under Dr. Manis—that he has made it clear in class that evolution is a fact, and that although 'some outsiders' (to use his language to his class) have tried to keep him from teaching evolution, they (the outsiders) will not succeed. Why is this being allowed to continue?!

"Third, why is it that in the past, teacher evaluation sheets (as completed by the students in any particular class) have always been **unsigned**, yet in certain biology classes this past spring semester students (e.g., those in Dr. Manis' class) were told that they **had to sign** the evaluation forms before they could leave the classroom? Since when has Abilene Christian University removed the anonymity promised to students filling out teacher evaluation forms so as to ensure truthful answers and protect the students from possible retaliation by teachers (the kind of retaliation which Dr. Manis himself has already demonstrated by illegally lowering a student's class grade!)?

"Fourth, why is it that teachers under your direct guidance are being openly allowed to use books written by atheistic humanists/evolutionists which flagrantly belittle, demean, and denigrate the biblcal creation account? As you are now aware, I am clearly referring to Dr. Manis' use of the book edited by the famous humanist/evolutionist of Princeton University, Dr. Ashley Montagu, *Science and Creationism*. How is it that in a supposedly **Christian** University this can be allowed? And how is it that you, as Dean, can sit idly by and not only allow it, but defend those who do it? Is there so little respect for the verbal, plenary inspiration of the Scriptures left in the College of Science at Abilene Christian University that the very Dean of the College will acquiesce to such blatant abuse of the Word of God?

"Attached to this letter, Dr. Reeves, is a listing of several other questions which I am asking you to answer. Drs. Manis, Williams, and Little have adamantly refused to answer our questions. I have it on good report that their refusal is administration-directed, and that Vice-President Gray has instructed them not to answer our inquiries. No doubt Dr. Gray has given you the same command. Nevertheless, we are appending to this letter our appropriate questions—which one graduate faculty member at ACU was able to answer in less than 10 minutes—for you to answer. Your refusal to answer these questions will, of course, put you in the same camp with Drs. Manis, Williams, and Little. Each question is intended to elicit a simple 'yes' or 'no' response; however, should you feel that more is needed, please do not hesitate to append whatever response you feel is justified. We will eagerly await your response, as we are most anxious to see a solution to this problem, which is directly and adversely affecting the faith of young people studying with professors under your direction, and at a supposedly **Christian** University.

"As I close, I would like to make one thing crystal clear to you, and through you to Drs. Manis, Williams, Little, Gray, and eventually to Dr. Teague himself. Do not think that your refusal to respond to our letters, or to answer our questions, will be a solution to this problem. Do not deceive yourself into thinking that this problem will simply 'go away' if you will simply remain quiet and attempt to ignore our inquiries. **Nothing could be farther from the truth!** I want you, and all other parties at ACU involved, to clearly understand that we intend to pursue this matter until the professors, department heads, and yes, even the Dean involved fully repent. We will **not** sit quietly by and allow the souls of young people to be tainted, mis-directed, and possibly eternally damaged by the teaching of organic and/or theistic evolution by your faculty. I do not think I can make it any clearer to you than that.

Sincerely,
(signed) Bert Thompson, Ph.D.
Professor of Bible & Science
Alabama Christian School of Religion

"Attachment

"PS: Dr. Reeves, I have it in print, and from an authoritative source at the University, that you are now on record as stating that if it can be fully documented that professors under your direction **are**, in fact, teaching evolution, they will be terminated in their positions at Abilene Christian University. I commend you for that stand, if you are indeed sincere in your statements. Furthermore, I now stand ready to fully document to you that indeed, Drs. Manis and Williams **are** teaching evolution to students at Abilene Christian University. I am now requesting, via this letter, a meeting with you in order to provide you with that documentation. Any refusal to allow me to take you up on your offer would, of course, seriously damage your credibility. I will, therefore, look forward to a letter from you, suggesting a time and place for our meeting so that you can examine the documentation I am prepared to provide.

PPS: Questions 40-43 will be of special interest to you as Dean.

[Questions 1-18 are exactly the same as questions 1-18 in the Manis, Williams, and Little letters. Questions 19-21 are exactly the same as questions 19-21 in Dr. Little's letter previously. Questions 22-43 are new and/or different and are reproduced below.]

_____ 22. Do you now teach, or have you ever taught, theistic evolution (i.e., that the theory of evolution as taught in most scientific circles today may be accepted at the same time as belief in God) in your classes at Abilene Christian University?

_____ 23. Are you now refuting, or have you refuted, the General Theory of Evolution (i.e., organic evolution) in your classes, in an attempt to make certain that your students understand it is false, and not to be accepted?

_____ 24. Are you now presenting, or have you presented, any of the evidence from the various fields of science which help to establish the creation model as the superior model of origins?

_____ 25. Are you now presenting, or have you presented, material in your classes **against** the creation model of origins?

_____ 26. To your knowledge, are any of the professors under your immediate direction in the Department of Biology at Abilene Christian University publicly teaching in their classes (and advocating that their students accept as a factual, correct account for the origin of the universe and life forms in that universe) either organic evolution or theistic evolution?

_____ 27. If it could be proven to you that certain professors under your direction, as Dean, and in the Biology Department for which you have responsibility, **are** teaching and advocating the acceptance of either organic evolution or theistic evolution, would you take appropriate administrative steps to see to it that these men were reprimanded, repented, and did not continue such teachings?

_____ 28. If it could be proven to you that certain professors under your direction, as Dean of the College of Natural and Applied Sciences, **are** teaching and advocating the acceptance of either organic evolution or theistic evolution, would you allow such teaching to continue?

_____ 29. One of the professors under your direction, Dr. Archie Manis, has been using as a textbook for one of the courses he teaches the blatantly anti-creationist book, *Science and Creationism*, edited by the famous evolutionist/humanist, Dr. Ashley

Montagu. Were you aware, prior to the beginnings of our correspondence with professors at ACU, of Dr. Manis' use of this textbook in his biology classes?

_____ 30. If your answer to question #29 above is 'yes,' were you aware of the fact that the Montagu book openly attacks the biblical doctrines of creation, God, etc.?

_____ 31. If your answer to question #30 above was 'yes,' did you approve the use of the book anyway?

_____ 32. If your answer to question #29 above was 'no,' and you were not aware of the use of the Montagu textbook in an ACU biology class, once you **were** made aware of the use of such a book (e.g., through our correspondence) did you then initiate steps to see to it that the book was either removed from the classroom, or that the anti-creation, anti-God concepts which the book presents were openly **refuted** in the classroom?

_____ 33. Is it true that at the end of the spring semester in 1985 certain professors in the Department of Biology at Abilene Christian University handed out a teacher-evaluation form to certain (or all) classes which **had** to be signed by the students completing it, and which contained the following statements: 'As you are undoubtedly aware, the subject of evolution can be a sensitive issue in a Christian college context. In view of the fact that the subject has been an integral part of this course, we would appreciate your opinions as they relate to the presentation of the material in this class. The professor will not have access to your response until after grades have been turned in.'?

_____ 34. **Has** evolution been taught 'as an integral part' of biology classes at Abilene Christian University, as the teacher-evaluation form mentioned in question #33 above so states?

_____ 35. Has it been standard procedure at Abilene Christian University in the past to **require** that students

sign their teacher-evaluation forms?

_____ 36. If the answer to question #35 above is 'no,' was the **requirement** that students in certain biology classes **sign** their teacher-evaluation forms an attempt on the part of certain professors or certain administrators to 'identify' certain students who have publicly or privately opposed the teaching of evolution on the campus at Abilene Christain University?

_____ 37. To your knowledge, have any students (i.e., one or more) made attempts to discuss the teaching of evolution or theistic evolution as factual in the Department of Biology at Abilene Christian University with you or any other administrator?

_____ 38. Are you, as Dean of the College of Natural and Applied Sciences, aware of the fact that Dr. Archie Manis has been handing out in his classes reprints from anti-creationists literature (e.g., chapters from Dr. Philip Kitcher's book, _Abusing Science: The Case Against Creationism_) and urging the students to accept as correct the positions against creationism as advocated by such anti-creationist authors?

_____ 39. If your answer to question #38 above is 'no,' now that you are aware that such is occurring, will you allow it to continue?

_____ 40. Did you personally make the statement to at least one ACU faculty member that if it could be adequately proven to you that Drs. Manis and Williams **are** teaching evolution, they would be fired from their positions with the University?

_____ 41. Would you be willing, as Dean, to examine evidence presented to you by me which would establish the fact that Drs. Manis and Williams **are** teaching evolution as factual to the students in their classes at Abilene Christian University?

_____ 42. Is it correct that Vice-President Gray has directed all parties involved in this controversy **not** to respond to my letters, but rather to ignore my inquiries into this matter?

_____ 43. If you personally accept and/or teach any form of evolution or theistic evolution, or are willing to let it be advocated as correct in the College of Natural and Applied Sciences at Abilene Christian University, would you be willing to publicly debate your position in order to establish it as correct and true?"

At this point we might mention that shortly before we penned our letter to Dean Reeves, one of the students in the biology department, who had taken classes under Drs. Manis and Williams during the spring, 1985 semester wrote calling our attention to an unusual "occurrence" at the end of that semester. As is the custom, a "teacher evaluation form" was handed to the students, so that they could "evaluate" the biology department professors and their teaching. But this "evaluation form" had been "modified." Included in the form was the following statement: "As you are undoubtedly aware, the subject of evolution can be a sensitive issue in a Christian college context. In view of the fact that the subject has been **an integral part of this course**, we would appreciate your opinions as they relate to the presentation of the material in this class. The professor will not have access to your response until after grades have been turned in." Consider the following important points. (A) Notice the **admission** that the teaching of evolution has been "an integral part of this course." (B) Notice that the statement is made that "the professor will not have access to your response until after grades have been turned in." Why would it matter if the professor(s) had access to the evaluation forms **before** grades had been turned in—unless it **had** become apparent that certain doctors were "doctoring" certain grades!? Moreover, in the past, teacher evaluation forms had been completely anonymous. But not in this case! As unbelievable as it is, the students **were forced to sign the teacher evaluation forms**, and were told that they **could not leave the room until they had both completed and signed the form**. To our knowledge (based on our research) never in the history of Abilene Christian University have students been **required** (much less **forced**) to sign teacher evaluation forms. Now, suddenly, without notice, students (and apparently only in the biology department) are being **required** both to **sign** the teacher evaluation form, and to **answer a specific question** regarding the "teaching of the subject of evolution." How, we ask, can this be happening on the campus of a **Christian** college or university? Further, what could possibly be the purpose behind such heretofore unheard of antics?! Is it possible that the professors, and their immediate superiors (Department Head, Dean, et al.) are attempting to "gather documentation" (even if **forced**) to "cover their trails" regarding the teaching of evolution? And, of course, the question must be asked: When a student is **forced** to sign an evaluation, and his **name** is on it **prior** to the grade for the course being turned in, what kind of "honest" evaluation does the University actually think it is likely to receive? There is a subtle intimidation regardless of "promises" previously made by University officials. And surely the reader is wondering **why** it was specifically stated that the professor would not have access to the evaluation until **after** grades had been turned in. Is there a hint of possible impropriety here? Considering Mark Scott's case, the question almost seems to answer itself, doesn't it?

Second, the reader is asked to notice the "PS" at the end of the letter to Dean Reeves. We stated that we had it, **in print**, from an authoritative source at the University that if it could be fully documented to Dr. Reeves that Manis and Williams **were**, in fact, teaching evolution as factual, they would not **be** fired, they **already are** fired. As the reader will learn shortly, that statement **was** made by Dean Reeves, and was acknowledged by him in a meeting on the University's campus on September 13, 1985—the same day that incontrovertible evidence was presented proving beyond the shadow of a doubt that the two professors were, and are, teaching evolution as factual to their students. Alas, however, Dean Reeves has not kept his word, and apparently has no intention of doing so. Considering some of the other "promises" from ACU administrators which have never been kept, it is not exactly the "shock of the century" that Dean Reeves has ignored this pledge. Evidence of this statement is provided in the information which follows.

To no one's great surprise, our letter to Dean Reeves was

completely ignored, and went totally unanswered. But, in keeping with our promise to follow the appropriate "chain of command" at ACU, we were preparing to write the President of the University, Bill Teague, concerning these matters (not that we thought, by this time, that it would do any good, but because we had given our word that we would follow through on this thing in a proper manner). However, shortly before our letter to President Teague was formulated, several events transpired which proved to be of importance in this controversy.

First, a copy of a letter written to President Teague by J.R. Clark, M.D. of Waxahachie, Texas was sent to us by Dr. Clark himself. Dr. Clark had heard of the problem at ACU's biology department, and having children of college-age, he wrote (on July 8, 1985) to Dr. Teague to inquire about the situation. On July 24, 1985 Teague responded to Dr. Clark's inquiry. President Teague's comments in his letter were, in part, as follows: "Dear Dr. Clark: Your letter has been received. The allegations are specious. . . .Please pray for us as we teach God's word even though opposed by hedonists, humanists, and relative [sic.] well-intentioned critics whose zeal is not always according to knowledge. . . .Conclusions based upon partial knowledge through one or two students are always suspect. We shall continue to pray for those individuals in our brotherhood who believe that some organization outside the church is needed to maintain maturity of the church. While we pray for them, we will not encourage them by completeing questionnaires." From these statements, and others which were sent to us by people who had also written President Teague, it became crystal clear that from the highest administrative official to the lowest staff member, the University was determined to both ignore and cover up the scandalous teachings of its biology professors. As Dr. Clark noted in his reply to President Teague's letter, if ACU had received a questionnaire from some brotherhood publication inquiring about the demographics of the student body, or some other salient point, the University would gladly have responded. But suddenly when the University receives a questionnaire about its **doctrinal stance**, the inquiry is altogether ignored. One cannot but wonder, "Why?".

Second, we received an urgent telephone call from Mark Scott the weekend before the fall, 1985 semester was to begin at Abilene Christian University. Mark had gone by the biology department in order to pick up the class cards which would allow him to register, and the departmental secretary promptly informed him that **his registration had been blocked!** When Mark inquired as to what that meant, the secretary told him that the Department Head, Dr. John Little, had given strict instructions that Mark Scott was not to be allowed to register for the fall semester. One can well imagine the surprise, and shock, that ensued. Here is a student who has returned to complete his senior year, and the Department Head has blocked that student's registration in courses which the student **must** have in order to complete his degree requirements so that he can graduate on time.

Upon learning that he had actually been blocked from registering for classes, Mark Scott inquired of the Department Head, Dr. John Little, as to **why** these instructions had been given. [NOTE: In some instances students are blocked from registration for non-payment of previous semesters' bills. This was **not** the case in this instance.] Dr. Little told Mark Scott outright that Drs. Manis and Williams did not want him in their classes, and, at their request, he had been refused permission to register. Mark called our office to inform us of these new developments, and to tell us that he was on his way to visit with Dr. C.G. Gray, Vice-President for Academic Affairs, in order to protest this intrusion into his school rights. And what was the outcome of this scenario? Mark made it abundantly clear to the University officials that they had two choices: (A) either allow him to register for his biology courses—which he had every right to do, or; (B) refuse him permission, in which case he would promptly contact the accrediting association in charge of granting ACU the status as an "accredited" university, which it now enjoys. Mark made it clear that he would file a formal complaint against the University for its refusal to allow a student the right to enroll and matriculate, as per its charter. Apparently the University believed him, because he was eventually allowed to enroll for his senior year, but **only** after Dr. C.G. Gray called him into his office and "scolded" him, reminding him that he was not to "cause any trouble" for the two professors (Manis and Williams) as he had done the semester before. Subsequently, Mark was allowed to enroll, but **only** after threatening to file a formal complaint against the University with its accrediting association. All of this—at a supposedly "Christian" university! [NOTE: Mark thought this settled the matter. He was wrong. He would later have his pre-registration for his last semester at ACU blocked by Dr. Gray himself.]

The third event to transpire amidst all of this was perhaps the most startling—and the most important. For several months prior to this time, this writer had been scheduled to hold a creation/evolution seminar at the 5th & Grape Street Church of Christ in Abilene, Texas (the seminar, incidentally, was scheduled long before any of the events regarding the teaching of evolution at ACU took place). The seminar was to be held at the Grape Street building the weekend of September 13-15, 1985. The Grape Street elders had appointed one of the deacons, Stan Harvey, to take care of the advertising. Stan outdid himself, in more ways than even he could know. Here is the reason for that statement. In the August 15, 1985 issue of the *Gospel Advocate* (p 491) there was a large, 3/4-page advertisement of the upcoming seminar. The advertisement contained a picture of the speaker, as well as the entire schedule of lectures for the weekend series. All arrangements for such advertising are taken care of by the local congregation, and not by our office. This is standard procedure. **We** knew that; apparently the people at ACU **did not**! They saw the huge box ad in the August 15 issue of the *Advocate*, and **assumed** (wrongly, I might add) that I had placed the ad in the journal, knowing that they would see it, and that it was my way of informing them that I was coming to Abilene in order to "make public" the entire sordid affair (regarding the teaching of evolution) at ACU. How do I know this? A word of explanation is certainly in order.

On September 6, 1985—one week to the day before I was to leave for Abilene—Dr. C.G. Gray, Vice-President for Academic Affairs at ACU, telephoned me at exactly 8:00 A.M. at my office in Montgomery. [NOTE: This is the first contact with anyone from ACU that we had had since April 12, 1985 when Dr. Reeves wrote his short, three-paragraph letter to appease us.] Needless to say, I was shocked that ACU had finally broken the "code of silence" which had been imposed on the University community by the Board of Trustees. I asked Dr. Gray ₁why he happened to be calling now, after ignoring my letters for seven long months. He quickly told me that University officials had seen the ads I had placed in the *Gospel Advocate*, and that they wanted to know if I would meet with them **before** I publicized these matters in the Grape Street seminar. One might well imagine the smile that crossed my face as I listened to Dr. Gray over the telephone. For seven long months I had attempted to get answers to my questions—or even a communication of any kind—and had received not a word. Now—because of a simple well-placed ad in the *Advocate* (an ad I had not even seen until just a few days earlier)—suddenly I was receiving personal calls from Vice-Presidents asking **me** to meet with **ACU**!? I told Dr. Gray, first, that I had nothing to do with the ad in the *Advocate*, but that the local congregation takes care of all advertising for the seminar. Further, I told him that I had **no intention** of saying anything regarding the ACU controversy during the Grape Street seminar. I informed him that I did not work that way, and that I had already explained to the ACU administration (via my letters) exactly how I intended to handle this controversy (i.e., through proper administrative channels). Third, I also told Dr. Gray that I intended to come by ACU and meet with school representatives while I was in Abilene **whether they had invited me or not**! I felt that since I was unable to get any response in any other way, perhaps dropping by their offices might do it! Dr. Gray asked me what time would be appropriate for the meeting, and I suggested sometime on Friday morning, September 13. He asked if 9:00 A.M. was acceptable, and I informed him that it was. The meeting was then set for that day and time. One week later, the meeting would, in fact, take place. Our intended letter (see above) to President Teague never materialized—due to the events that would transpire at ACU on September 13. It is now to that meeting that we turn our attention, because it represented a turning point of sorts in this controversy. However, before giving an in-depth account of what happened at that meeting, a moment's worth of additional research information is needed here.

On September 2, 1985 (four days before Dr. Gray's telephone call) I received a most unusual letter in the mail. The letter was hand-written, and was four (small) pages long. Here is the history behind the letter, and its contents. News regarding the ongoing controversy over evolution was beginning to get out—in spite of the University's best efforts to "keep the lid" on it. As unusual as it may seem, one of the places that heard of the problem was a small town in northern Texas by the name of Texline. The preacher in the local Church of Christ is John Scott [no relation to Mark]. About a year ago, I held a creation/evolution seminar at the Texline congregation. I had not personally informed the Texline congregation about this problem. The information had gotten to them from another source. A lady from the congregation, Mrs. Rowena Lobley, wrote me a most interesting letter. Here is its content, in part:

"Dear Dr. Thompson:

We are very interested and concerned about evolution being taught at ACU. Let me start at the beginning. Our daughter, Brenda Lobley, is in her second year of medical school in San Antonio. She graduated magna cum laude from ACU in 1984. A couple of years ago, she and I had a talk that alarmed me very much. She was very confused about evolution. Needless to say, I never dreamed this could happen at ACU. Jerry, my husband, graduated from ACC in 1959. I attented 3 semesters. I called Dr. John Little [Chairman, biology department—BT]. He told me Dr. Manis was an elder and thought he was solid. I called Dr. Manis. He didn't return my call and I let it drop. I talked to John [Scott] up there then. When we didn't discuss it again with Brenda for awhile, I didn't think much more about it. Then Wednesday night we heard about your attempts to ask some questions and the way you have been treated. I called Brenda night before last. She said her troubles started with Dr. Kenneth Williams. She had **nothing** good to say

-66-

about him. Then, she admitted she was still confused but she didn't worry with it because she isn't confronted with it. Needless to say, I am furious!!—and not at Brenda. We are praying for this meeting. We pray it can be Christ-like and get to the truth. I think we already know what that is. Brenda made the comment that if ACU doesn't teach evolution it will lose credibility with the 'scientific community.' She probably hit the nail on the head. We are with you all the way. I, or we, have written letters to: Dr. John Stevens, Dr. Gray, Dr. Reeves, Dr. Little, Dr. Bill Teague, Ray McGlothlin. . . .Thank you for all of your efforts. Let us know the outcome. We are praying for you and the others that this can be settled.

(signed) Yours Truly, Rowena (Sheets) Lobley."

The reader can well imagine the impact such a letter had. While Dr. Reeves attempts to "paper over" the situation with a three-paragraph letter assuring us that "all is well in Zion," suddenly we begin getting letters such as this to the effect that not only are things not well **now**, but in fact they have not been well for quite some time! [NOTE: This letter from Mrs. Lobley is only one of such instances where the teaching of evolution at ACU—in some cases going as far back as 1972—has been documented. Additional evidence to follow.] Upon receiving the letter from Mrs. Lobley, I picked up the telephone and called her. I spoke with both her and her husband for quite some time. During our conversation, she indicated to me (and she has indicated to others since that time, including certain ACU officials) that during her conversation with Brenda she specifically asked if Brenda's instructors (Drs. Manis and Williams) **refuted** evolution when they presented it. Brenda told her mother that quite the contrary, it was presented as **fact**, and that is was **never** refuted in class. But more than that, Brenda showed her mother the book which they were required to read. Mrs. Lobley pulled it from the bookshelf in her home the night of our phone conversation, and read the title and author to me. The author of the book (and be reminded that this is the book **required** by Dr.Manis in his seminar class)was Dr. Stephen

J. Gould (that's right, the Marxist/evolutionist from Harvard). The book was entitled *Ever Since Darwin*. I have the book in my personal library, and know all-too-well its contents. It is a collection of essays from Dr. Gould's column in the famous science magazine, *Natural History*. Each essay is a **defense** of evolution, and many of the essays are openly critical of the Bible, God, and especially creationism. This was the book **required** by Dr. Manis of his students in his biology seminar class in the spring of 1984.

I asked Mrs. Lobley if it would be acceptable for me to call Brenda, and talk to her personally. She stated that it would be fine. On Thursday evening, September 12, I called Brenda from my motel room in Abilene, Texas (I flew in a day early in order to prepare for the Friday morning meeting with ACU officials). My phone conversation with Brenda (in San Antonio) lasted approximately 20-30 minutes, from 11:30 P.M. that evening until almost midnight. During the course of our conversation, I asked Brenda several questions. Was she taught evolution as a **fact**? Yes, she stated, most definitely. Was evolution ever **refuted**? Absolutely not, she said. Was the book, *Ever Since Darwin*, by Gould **required** reading? Yes, she stated, it was. Were the concepts which the book presents **refuted** by Dr. Manis in the class? No, she said, they were not. Were Drs. Manis and Williams, in her estimation, out-and-out theistic evolutionists? Yes, she said, they were. [NOTE: Let the reader be reminded that we are here dealing with a magna cum laude graduate from the ACU biology department and a young lady who **was** pre-med and who is **now** in medical school.] Was she taught evolution as **fact** by Dr. Williams in the class(es) she took under him? Most definitely, she stated. Remembering her mother's statement in the letter which I had received just a few days before, I asked Brenda what her mother meant when she said that Brenda "has absolutely **nothing** good to say about" Dr. Kenneth Williams. Brenda told me quite plainly that she "was not even sure the man believed in God, to be quite honest." Upon hearing that statement, I remembered a specific letter that I had received about five months earlier from a student at ACU. I pulled that letter from my briefcase and read the following statement: "Williams' teaching on evolution is so common that some students I have talked to told me they used to get mad when he taught evolution, and I suggested that they tell Dean Reeves about it, but they just don't care anymore now. One girl said she just gave up and figured Williams was an 'atheist.' " Not a very pretty picture of a Christian professor, is it? One girl from two years back states that she is not even sure he believes in God. Yet another girl, from just a few months ago, states that she figures he is just "an atheist" from the things he teaches. How, one might ask, can all of this be happening in a **Christian** university environment?

But there is more! Just prior to my meeting with ACU officials on September 13, 1985 I learned of two additional significant events. They were, in fact, related. First, I learned that Dr. Archie Manis used as his text material for his summer, 1985 freshman biology course the new "Life on Earth" materials, prepared by the famous British evolutionist, David Attenborough. Not only did Dr. Manis use the written materials, but he had his students watch the film series which has been prepared to go along with the textual materials. Perhaps the reader would be interested in hearing some of the section titles from the written materials: (A) The First Forests; (B) Conquest of the Waters; (C) The Invasion of the Land; (D) Lords of the Air; (E) The Rise of the Mammals; (F) The Hunters and the Hunted; (G) Life in the Trees; (H) The Compulsive Communicators. Enough said!

Second, and much more important, is this little pearl. On the first day of the freshman biology class, Dr. Manis waltzed into the room and (according to testimony we have) practically the first words out of his mouth were these: "There are some people 'outside' the University community who are trying to tell me what I can and cannot teach. But they won't succeed. I'm an elder in the church, and I believe in evolution. I'm going to teach it to you, and you are going to believe it as well." Can you imagine? A man who is supposedly an elder in the church, and a professor at a **Christian** university, walks into his **freshman** biology class and "informs" them that he "believes in evolution" and they are going to learn it and believe in it as well?! What next? Well, consider this. One of the students in that class was a young lady (a junior scholar, in fact) by the name of Lisa Fitts. Lisa became upset at Dr. Manis' remarks, and went to tell the Vice-President for Academic Affairs, Dr. C.G. Gray, about the incident. However, Dr. Gray was not in the office at the time, so she asked to see Dr. Robert Hunter, Vice-President of the University. Upon learning why Lisa wanted to visit with him, Dr. Hunter suggested (is this intimidation???) that the meeting between them be tape-recorded. One might well imagine his surprise when she quickly agreed! Lisa informed Dr. Hunter what Dr. Manis said, and the conversation **was** tape-recorded! Shortly after that we learned that several members of the ACU administration (including Dean Reeves, Dr. Gray, et al.) had, in fact, listened to that taped conversation!!

With these pieces of information (and several others) safely "tucked away" and at my disposal, I made preparations to attend the meeting the morning of September 13, 1985.

Showdown In Abilene

"Personally, I heard brother Ken Williams give a speech to the faculty some five years ago or so. His speech was peppered throughout with evolutionary and uniformitarian terminology. I marked down then in my mind that he accepted and believed far more of the theory of evolution than was healthy. I shared my concern with two or three of the administrators, but so far as I know, nothing was ever pursued concerning the matter."

—Dr. Furman Kearley
Editor, **Gospel Advocate**, Formerly
Director of Graduate Bible Studies,
Abilene Christian University; in a
letter to Mr. Dub Orr, ACU Board
member, (November 11, 1985, p 3)

"Biological evolution is a part of the evolution of the cosmos. The rise and development of mankind are a part of the story of biological evolution. Man cannot reach a valid understanding of his own nature without a knowledge of his own biological background. It may, then, be that the study of evolutionary biology is the most important practical endeavor open to the human mind. Accordingly, an effort is being made in this book to show to the student that biology is not only a craft which is

interesting to technicians and devotees but also a part of the fabric of modern humanistic thought."
—Dr. Theodosius Dobzhansky
Foremost evolutionary geneticist
In: **Evolution, Genetics, and Man**
Textbook required by Dr. Kenneth
Williams for his biology seminar
class (Bio. 4196), spring, 1972

At exactly 9:00 o'clock on the morning of September 13, 1985 my meeting with ACU officials did take place in the President's conference room in the Administration building on campus. Present at this gathering were the following individuals representing ACU: (A) Dr. C.G. Gray, Vice-President for Academic Affairs; (B) Dr. Ian Fair, Dean of the College of Biblical Studies; (C) Dr. Perry Reeves, Dean of the College of Natural and Applied Sciences; (D) Mr. Dub Orr, member of and representing the ACU Board of Trustees. Accompanying me to the meeting was Michael Seale, a young man involved part-time in the work at Apologetics Press, Inc. Sitting in on the meeting, at my request, was an "independent" or "neutral" witness, Mr. James D. Willeford, one of the elders of the 5th & Grape Street Church of Christ. I felt that, considering the importance of this meeting and the topics to be discussed, it would be best for both sides if a "neutral" witness were present. That way, if there was any doubt at a later point in time regarding the things said in the meeting, there would be someone to whom both sides could turn as an "arbitrator." As it turns out, the wisdom of that suggestion proved quite invaluable.

The meeting with the ACU officials lasted approximately 2½ hours—from 9:00 A.M. until 11:30 A.M. Rather than relying on this writer for **his** estimation of what happened in that meeting, the reader is asked instead to examine the following statement as attested to by James D. Willeford, the "neutral" or "independent" witness. Brother Willeford was not present to represent **either** side. His testimony of what occurred in that particular meeting should be viewed in light of that fact. But before introducing this document, I would like to make mention of something that the reader will no doubt find conspicuously **absent** from the record of the meeting. In fact, the reader may already have "picked up" on this particular point. I have already listed those members of the ACU administration who were present at this meeting. But notice who was **not** there. Neither Dr. Manis nor Dr. Williams was at the meeting. When Dr. Gray called me on September 6, I specifically asked that Manis and Williams attend the meeting, so that they could "face their accuser" as it were. Upon my arrival at the meeting, their absence was conspicuous. I inquired as to why these two professors were not present. Imagine my surprise when Mr. Orr, the Board member, spoke up to say that the ACU administration felt that it was best that they not be there. When I inquired as to why, the answer I received was shocking indeed. Mr. Orr said that Archie Manis was "red-headed and hot-tempered, and might do something violent" if allowed to come to the meeting. And **this** is the man who is an elder at the Baker Heights congregation in Abilene?! How is it possible for a man who is allegedly an elder to have such a characteristic? I thought that the Bible taught that an elder must be, among other things, **temperate** and "not soon angry"?! In any case, Mr. Orr explained that the ACU administration had gone to great lengths to "keep the professors from me." Little wonder I couldn't get an answer to a letter; I couldn't even come to their own city and get them to meet with me **in person**! As I thought over these things while sitting in the meeting, and as I have continued to run them through my mind since, one haunting question keeps nagging at me: if they refuse to answer my letters, will not answer my questions regarding their teachings, and are afraid to meet me in a face-to-face confrontation, is it possible —just possible—that they have something to hide?! I honestly think the question answers itself.

Below is a detailed summary of the meeting in which I participated on September 13 along with ACU administration officials. I will let the reader judge for himself the things herein recorded. [NOTE: The original document, as prepared from notes and eyewitness testimony, and signed by brother Willeford, is on file in our office.]

REPORT AND SUMMARY OF A MEETING BETWEEN DR. BERT THOMPSON AND ABILENE CHRISTIAN UNIVERSITY REPRESENTATIVES ON SEPTEMBER 13, 1985

During the weekend of September 13-15, 1985, the 5th & Grape Street Church of Christ in Abilene, Texas sponsored a seminar at its building, dealing with the current creation/ evolution controversy. The speaker for the weekend seminar was Dr. Bert Thompson of Montgomery, Alabama. Dr. Thompson had been invited to present the seminar in order to better inform the 5th & Grape membership of the present controversy, and in order to refute the false system of evolution and uphold the Genesis account of creation. In the opinion of the 5th & Grape eldership, by the conclusion of the weekend those two goals had been admirably achieved.

Prior to Dr. Thompson's arrival, the elders of the 5th & Grape Street congregation had heard from various sources about the current discussion between Dr. Thompson and representatives of Abilene Christian University (ACU) regarding the charges which Dr. Thompson, and others (including some students) had made concerning the teaching of evolution, or various forms of it, in certain classes in the biology department at the University. Upon his arrival in Abilene Thursday afternoon, September 12, the 5th & Grape elders requested that Dr. Thompson meet with them to discuss both the ACU controversy and the plans for the weekend seminar. During this session, Dr. Thompson informed the elders that on the following morning, September 13, at 9:00 A.M. he would be meeting with representatives of ACU in order to discuss the charges and possible solutions to the problem as it then existed. During the discussion with the eldership, Dr. Thompson suggested that it might be judicious for someone in a "neutral" position to accompany him to the meeting as an "independent" witness—a person who was extraneous to the current controversy, and not associated with him, or with ACU, in any way. The 5th & Grape Street elders, whose only desire is that Truth be upheld and that the Gospel of Christ be preached without compromise, agreed that such would be a wise action to follow. Dr. Thompson asked the convened eldership if one of the 5th & Grape elders might possibly attend the meeting the next morning with him. Several of the Grape Street elders offered to go as an "independent" witness, and after some few moments of discussion on the matter, it was decided that James D. Willeford would be the one to go with Dr. Thompson to the meeting.

On Friday morning, September 13, 1985 the meeting between Dr. Thompson and ACU representatives occurred as scheduled. The meeting was held in the President's Conference Room, with the following men present representing ACU: (1) Dr. C.G. Gray, Vice-President for Academic Affairs; (2) Dr. Perry Reeves, Dean of the College of Natural and Applied Sciences; (3) Dr. Ian Fair, Dean of the College of Bible; (4) Mr. Dub Orr, member of and representing the Board of Trustees of ACU. In attendance with Dr. Thompson was Michael Seale, who had accompanied him from Montgomery, Alabama. James D. Willeford was the "neutral" or "independent" witness present.

As the meeting began, Dr. Thompson asked for the floor, and was granted permission to speak. He indicated first that he was present representing only himself, and not the school for which he teaches, the Alabama Christian School of Religion in Montgomery, Alabama. He stated second that he wished the University officials to know that he had **not** come to Abilene to make any public statements regarding the controversy at ACU, and fully intended to confine himself to the creation/evolution issue during his lectures at the Grape Street congregation. It was not his intention, explained Dr. Thompson, to "use" the Grape Street pulpit in order to bring this matter to the public's attention, and he wanted the ACU officials to know that. Dr. Thompson stated that he fully intended to keep to his original agenda, as published in previous letters to the University. These statements were the exact statements which Dr. Thompson had just made the evening before in a meeting with the Grape Street elders.

At the beginning of the meeting, Mr. Orr asked Dr. Thompson to please give some background information on himself, which he then did, including the fact that he was a 1971 ACU (then known as ACC) alumnus, having graduated with a B.S. degree in biology. He explained that he had completed the M.S. and Ph.D. degrees in microbiology from Texas

A&M University, and that he had taught at that institution for several years in the College of Veterinary Medicine. Dr. Thompson further explained that he now taught as a Professor at the Alabama Christian School of Religion under the direction of Dr. Rex A. Turner, Sr. and that he also travelled extensively—almost every weekend of the year—presenting seminars refuting evolution and upholding the Genesis account of creation as told in the Bible.

After that introduction, Dr. Ian Fair stated to Dr. Thompson that it was his conviction that Dr. Thompson had badly mishandled this inquiry from the very beginning, since he had not gone **personally**, as Matthew 18 directed, to the two professors involved. Dr. Fair was quite strong in his statement that as far as he was concerned, the entire affair, as it now existed, was due to the mishandling of matters by Dr. Thompson since he had disobeyed the biblical injunction in Matthew 18. Dr. Thompson quickly pointed out to Dr. Fair that he (Dr. Fair) had taken Matthew 18 out of its proper context. Matthew 18, Dr. Thompson pointed out, dealt with a brother who had sinned against a brother. Dr. Thompson pointed out very quickly that he had never accused either of the two professors of "sinning" against him. Dr. Fair stated that nevertheless, Matthew 18 was binding in this case. Dr. Thompson strongly disagreed, but then pointed out that he had, in fact, "gone to" the two professors—privately by means of his two letters dated March 27, 1985. Dr. Thompson asked Dr. Fair if an individual, separated from a brother in Christ by many miles, might "go to" the brother by letter or telephone? Dr. Fair said "No," that he had to go to him **personally**, in a **physical** way. Dr. Thompson pointed out that it must, then, have been the case that the apostle Paul "mishandled" the various cases with which he dealt in the New Testament, because in many of them he was unable to "go to" the brother (or brethren) personally, and thus chose to take care of the matter by letter!

Immediately after this confrontation, Dr. Thompson reminded those present that **he** was not the one "on trial" in the first place, but that **ACU was**. He then asked for a statement from the ACU representatives regarding the charges which he, and various students, had made to the effect that Drs. Archie Manis and Kenneth Williams were teaching either theistic or organic evolution (as factual, true, and to be accepted) to the students in their respective classes. At that point, Dr. Gray spoke up and stated that the University flatly denied such allegations, and considered them to be completely false. Dr. Thompson then asked Dr. Gray, and the other men present in the room, if they were **absolutely certain** that this was the position they wished to defend; he offered them one last chance to recant and admit that evolution and/or theistic evolution was/were being taught. Dr. Gray stood firm, and stated that the University denied such. Dr. Thompson then requested the floor, and was granted, at his request, uninterrupted speaking time. At that time, he opened his briefcase and pulled from it various documents, from which he read. The first document was entitled "Evolution Notes" and was authored by Dr. Archie Manis. One of the points which Dr. Thompson read from the photocopied handout (used by Dr. Manis in his biology seminar class) stated:

> "Evolution's history and methodology will continue to feed debates for generations, but the **fact** of evolution is **beyond dispute**. The concept is **rational, scientific, and supported by an overwhelming mass of evidence** from past and present."

Dr. Thompson then read from Dr. Manis' handout entitled, "Research in Genesis" the following statement:

> "Discuss the differences between the two '**creation hymns**' (5 and 6 above). Are these two accounts of the same creation story, or is this repetition with a change in sequence?"

Dr. Thompson then produced a photocopy, as handed out in class to the students by Dr. Manis, of the first page of the Bible (Genesis 1 & 2). In the margin, in Dr. Manis' own handwriting, was written, "Creation Hymn, Myth." Dr. Thompson reminded those present that this was the professor's **own handwriting** and that this material, labeling the first chapters of Genesis a "myth," was **handed out in class**. Further, Dr. Thompson then inquired if the ACU representatives knew of, and agreed with, the textbook that Dr. Manis had used in his class? That book, a copy of which Dr. Thompson produced (complete with the "ACU Bookstore" sticker on the frontispiece) was *Science and Creationism*, edited by Ashley Montagu, the famous evolutionist/humanist (as Dr. Thompson pointed out) from Princeton University. Dr. Thompson read three quotations from the book, as used by Dr. Manis in his biology class. One of the quotations read as follows:

> "Evolution is a **fact**, not a theory. It once was a theory, but today, as a consequence of observation and testing it is probably the **best authenticated actuality known to science**. There are theories concerning the mechanisms of evolution, but **no competent student doubts the reality of evolution**" (p 13).

Dr. Thompson read the second quotation, which stated:

> ". . .whatever the historical antecedents of Genesis, it represents **but one of innumerable creation myths** which different people at different times have **invented** in order to account for the manner in which Earth and everything upon it came into being" (p 6).

Dr. Thompson also quoted the introductory statement to the volume:

> "The god who is reputed to have created fleas to keep dogs from moping over their situation must also have created fundamentalists to keep rationalists from getting flabby. Let us be duly thankful for our blessings" (p 3).

Dr. Thompson continued with other such materials, and after approximately 20-30 minutes of uninterrupted readings from the materials of the two professors, asked for an explanation of such materials. Mr. Orr spoke up to say that he was quite unable to explain these statements. Dr. Thompson then asked how he could state with such dogmatism that evolution

was not being taught to the students, when he could not even explain the statements to the contrary **from the professors' own materials?** Dr. Thompson asked Dr. Fair, Dean of the College of Bible, what he thought of the things he had heard. Dr. Fair asked to see the documents. Dr. Thompson handed them across the table, and after examination of them, Dr. Fair stated that in his opinion the statements made were (to use his exact phrase) "rotten." Dr. Thompson demanded explanation of these materials, which were, he noted, being taught at ACU to students under Drs. Manis and Williams. Finally, Dr. Gray spoke up to offer his explanation. He stated that the items were written by the professors **as if** they were evolutionists, so that the students could be exposed to how evolutionists think and write, but that these materials were then **refuted** in the classroom.

Dr. Thompson said that he was fully prepared to allow that that **might** be the case, and that it would certainly be an easy thing for the University to prove. So, Dr. Thompson asked Dr. Gray to provide him with the following items: (A) a list of the Scripture references used by the professors in the classes to refute the evolution-oriented materials, and to teach the correct view as presented in Genesis 1; (B) a list of the evidences from the various fields of science which both refuted evolution and showed creation to be the only logical alternative regarding origins; (C) a list of the **creationist** books used in the professors' classes, since books like the one by Montagu were openly used in class; (D) a copy of the bibliographies of **creationist** books handed out in class to which the students had been referred for additional reading; (E) a copy of the professors' "Creation Notes" or something akin to them, which gave as much time to refuting evolution as the "Evolution Notes" written by Dr. Manis did in **advocating evolution**.

Dr. Gray stated that he did not have any such items. Dr. Thompson quickly replied that he **knew** Dr. Gray did not have these items, because they **did not exist!** Dr. Thompson stated that before he came to the meeting on this Friday morning, he had "done his homework" and knew full-well that the professors never gave "equal time" to creation, but instead, taught evolution and only evolution, **without any rebuttal whatsoever**.

Dr. Thompson then asked Dr. Gray if the following incident had indeed occurred during the summer (1985) session at ACU. Did Dr. Archie Manis walk into his freshman biology class on the first day of class and make a statement that went something like this: "There are some on the outside of the University community who think that they can tell us what to teach, but they are wrong. I am an elder in the church, and I believe in evolution. I'm going to teach it to you, and you are going to believe it as well." Dr. Thompson stated that before Dr. Gray answered he should know that Dr. Thompson had done his homework on this particular item as well. Dr. Thompson stated that he knew, in fact, that one particular student (a girl) had become so upset by these statements that she went to Dr. Robert Hunter, Vice-President of the University, to complain about the things Dr. Manis had said. Dr. Hunter, in what might be interpreted as an attempt to "intimidate" the young lady, suggested that the conversation be tape-recorded. The young lady (whose name Dr. Thompson provided, by the way) quickly **agreed**, and the conversation **was taped**. Dr. Thompson asked Dr. Gray—knowing that he had heard the tape—if this incident **had** happened. Dr. Gray said that there was a tape in existence, but that nothing like what Dr. Thompson had just said was on that tape. At this point, Dr. Reeves, Dean of the College of Natural and Applied Sciences, leaned over and said, "Dr. Gray, it **is** on the tape, and you **know** it." Dr. Thompson asked for an explanation of such a statement, made by a man who is supposedly an elder in the church, and an ACU professor.

Dr. Perry Reeves stated that what Dr. Manis meant was that he would teach "natural selection." Dr. Thompson responded that a man with a Ph.D. in the biological sciences, and especially a Christian and elder in the church, should certainly know better than to walk into a classroom of impressionable young minds and say he was "going to teach them evolution" when in reality he meant only "natural selection." Dr. Thompson stated that he did **not** accept that explanation in any form. Dr. Thompson then turned to Dr. Fair and asked him what he thought of Dr. Manis' choice of words, in his statement to the class that he was going to "teach them evolution." Dr. Fair remarked that the choice of words was "pathetic."

Dr. Thompson then asked the ACU representatives in the room if they had not, in fact, just recently received a letter from Mrs. Rowena Lobley of Texline, Texas concerning the teaching of evolution by Drs. Manis and Williams to her daughter, Brenda, while she was at ACU two years ago? Before allowing the ACU representatives to answer, Dr. Thompson said that he wanted to warn them that he not only had a copy of the letter from Mrs. Lobley to the University, but that just the very night before this meeting, at approximately 11:30 P.M. (Thursday, September 12) he had spoken both with Mrs. Lobley in Texline and with Brenda, her daughter, who is now in medical school in San Antonio, Texas. Dr. Thompson asked the University officials if Mrs. Lobley had—true to her claim— written the University even earlier (more than a year earlier) to complain about the teaching of evolution by Drs. Manis and Williams in the classes which her daughter was having to take. Dr. Thompson asked those present if it was not true that Mrs. Lobley made it clear, in both communications with the University, that her daughter had been taught evolution by these two professors **without any refutation of it**. Dr. Thompson also asked the University officials if Mrs. Lobley had explained to them that because of this very situation her daughter had had, and was still having, severe "faith problems" regarding evolution and creation. Further, Dr. Thompson asked if the University officials were aware that the book used by Dr. Manis in teaching Mrs. Lobley's daughter evolution (along with all the other students in the class) was authored by the famed Marxist/evolutionist of Harvard University, Dr. Stephen Jay Gould and if they were aware that the book was completely anti-God, anti-creation, anti-religion, and anti-Bible. Dr. Thompson asked the officials why something was not done years ago when these complaints were first made known to the University by concerned parents such as Mr. & Mrs. Lobley. Dr. Thompson expressed his dismay at the fact that this situation—where men who are allegedly Christians violate the precious trust given to them by parents to train their children in the ways of the Bible and instead teach the children nothing but atheistic theories such as evolution— has apparently been going on for a long, long time. At this time, Dr. Thompson made the following statement to the University officials present: "Brethren, you have a **serious problem** here at this University in the biology department. You have men who are out-and-out theistic evolutionists teaching children sent here by parents who have entrusted you with their most precious possession—their own children. These men have violated and prostituted that trust, and I am therefore calling on you to correct the situation via appropriate measures."

Dr. Gray admitted that indeed, the University **had** received such letters from Mrs. Lobley, and that the University was looking into the situation. Mr. Orr spoke up and asked Dr. Thompson a pointed question. He said, "Are you asking us to **fire** these two men?" Dr. Thompson quickly responded. He said, "Brother Orr, I am asking you to **keep your word.**" Mr. Orr asked what Dr. Thompson meant by that statement. Dr. Thompson said that he would be happy to explain. Looking at Dr. Reeves, Dr. Thompson said, "Is it not true that several weeks ago, Dr. Furman Kearley, who was at that time Director of Graduate Bible Studies here at ACU, was in your office, speaking with you about these very matters? And is it not true, Dr. Reeves, that you told Dr. Kearley that if documentation could be provided which proved that these two men had, in fact, taught evolution, they would not be fired, they **already are** fired!?" Before Dr. Reeves could respond, Dr. Thompson said that he wanted to remind Dr. Reeves that he had in his briefcase a personal letter from Dr. Furman Kearley—with permission from Dr. Kearley to use it—which stated the exact words from Dr. Reeves. Dr. Reeves looked at Dr. Thompson across the table and said, "Yes, I **did** make those statements." Dr. Thompson looked at Mr. Orr, and said, "Brother Orr, your own Dean gave his word to a fellow Christian that these men would be fired if documentation could be provided that showed that they were teaching evolution. I have provided that documentation. Now, you **make your Dean keep his word!**"

After other discussion on these matters, Dr. Reeves asked Dr. Thompson if he didn't think it was a bit "odd" that the students hadn't said something before this? Dr. Thompson stated that he wasn't the least bit surprised, and for the following reason. Dr. Thompson addressed a question to Dr. Gray, as Vice-President. He asked if Dr. Manis had, in fact, actually **lowered** one student's grade from a "B" to a "C" and explained to the student that the grade was lowered "because you gave me so much trouble in class about teaching evolution." At first Dr. Gray denied that such ever took place, but Dr. Thompson threatened to pull the report card from his briefcase, and demand that it then be compared with what was then in the computer system under the student's grade report. Dr. Thompson stated that he had personally seen the computer report, where Dr. Gray's own command to change the grade back to the original "B" was logged in the computer's memory. Then Dr. Gray stated that yes, the incident had occurred, but that the problem had been corrected. Dr. Thompson then used this material to answer Dr. Reeves' question. No, said Dr. Thompson, he was not surprised at all that students would not "come forward" to complain. Look what happened to the one that did, stated Dr. Thompson!

After approximately two hours of such discussion, Dr. Thompson stated that he had not yet heard an adequate explanation of the evidences at-hand, and that he had not heard any potential solution. Mr. Orr spoke up to say that it was correct that the University's "aprons were not entirely clean," and that "some mistakes have been made." But Mr. Orr said, "We give you our word that it will be corrected."

Dr. Thompson said, "You have ignored my letters for seven months, you have attempted to perpetrate a cover-up, and I have caught you already in this meeting in severe discrepancies between the facts and the truth, and you want me to simply 'take your word' that the matters will be corrected. No sir."

Mr. Orr said, "Well, then, I suppose you have a suggested solution." Dr. Thompson replied that he did. Dr. Thompson said, "You have been telling me all morning that your two professors are innocent, and that they do not teach or believe in either organic or theistic evolution, so it should be no trouble at all for you to secure one document from each of the two professors which contains the following statements:

"1. I do not believe that Genesis 1-11 is a myth.

"2. I do believe that Genesis 1-11 is literal and historical, and will teach it as such to my classes.

"3. I **do not** believe in, or advocate that our students accept as factual and true, theistic evolution, progressive creation, mitigated evolution, etc.

"4. I **do** and **will** teach my students that theistic evolution, progressive creation, mitigated evolution, etc. are false, and **not** to be accepted as correct.

"5. I **do not** believe in organic evolution, and **will not** advocate it as factual, correct, and true in my classes.

"6. I **will** refute organic evolution in my classes, and **will** make certain my students understand that it is false.

"7. I **repent** of having taught evolution and/or theistic evolution to my classes in the past in such a way as to leave the impression through my oral and written presentations that evolution and/or theistic evolution are acceptable and may be believed by a faithful Christian."

Mr. Orr immediately spoke up to detest such a statement, suggesting that it would be an insult to the faculty members. Dr. Thompson pointed out that quite the contrary, it would be an instrument for their exoneration, since it would evidence their sincerity in wanting to correct their mistakes. Mr. Orr, and others present, including Dr. Gray, vehemently opposed such documents. Dr. Thompson pointed out that the University had two options. First, the University could provide the documents, as specified. Second, the University could refuse to supply the documents, as specified, and allow our brotherhood to be its judge, as the documentation presented in the meeting--and much more that had not even yet come to light—was published and made public. Dr. Thompson stated that unless the two documents, containing the items as he listed them in the meeting, were forthcoming, he would make the evidences he had shown in the meeting, and others that he had not revealed, public. Then, it would be up to the University "after the fact" to attempt to explain them. Dr. Thompson reminded the men that they were not even able to properly explain the documents when sitting directly across the table from their accuser, and with the documents in plain sight. How, he asked, would they ever be able to explain such information when it appeared in print before an inquiring brotherhood?

As the meeting ended, Dr. Thompson asked point-blank if the documents would be forthcoming. The men in the meeting gave Dr. Thompson their word as Christians that the documents would be provided as specified, but that they needed some time in order to get them together. Dr. Thompson said that he was more than willing to give them whatever time they needed, and asked how much time was necessary. They stated that they were unsure. Dr. Thompson then asked if six weeks— or until October 31, 1985—was enough time to have the documents (as specified) on his desk. Dr. Gray spoke up and indicated that six weeks was ample time. Before the meeting adjourned, Dr. Thompson made a closing statement in which he said that he wanted to make certain the items which he had listed were clearly understood as necessary to be in the statements signed by the two professors, and that he was putting—before everyone present—a disclaimer on the meeting. Dr. Thompson said that if the documents were not forthcoming by October 31, or if the documents did not contain the items which had been listed in the meeting (and which Dr. Fair had specifically written down in his notes), the University could view the meeting as never having taken place, and that the materials would be made public. Dr. Thompson asked everyone present if they understood completely. They indicated that they did. After additional discussion on some personal matters, the meeting was adjourned at approximately 11:30 A.M., or two-and-a-half hours after it commenced.

This document is based upon notes and eyewitness accounts from the meeting which occurred in the President's Conference Room on the campus of Abilene Christian University on September 13, 1985, and is, to my knowledge, accurate and properly represents the content of the meeting as it took place.

(signed) James D. Willeford

The brotherhood is deeply indebted to brother James D. Willeford for his willingness to both attend this meeting and to put into print a signed assessment of it. After the presentation of this summary, the following comments are in order.

One of the "red flag" issues throughout this entire ordeal concerns the textbook which Dr. Manis **required** his seminar students to both purchase and read. That book, *Science and Creationism*, edited by Dr. Ashley Montagu, is without a doubt one of the most venemous attacks upon creationism ever written. A quick glance at the list of contributors—Isaac Asimov, Stephen J. Gould, Garrett Hardin, Gunther Stent, Kenneth Boulding, George Marsden—would be enough to immediately call into question the wisdom of using such a book at all, much less on a Christian university campus! In the September 13 meeting, I read several quotations from the Montagu book (see page 78). However, at this point I would like to present additional documentation regarding the nature of this particular book, so that no one will be in doubt as to the intent of the book—the total and absolute destruction of any belief whatsoever in the divinely inspired account of creation. Consider, for example, the following statements by Dr. Stephen J. Gould:

> "Well, evolution is a theory. It is also a fact. . . .Humans evolved from ape-like ancestors whether they did so by Darwin's proposed mechanism or by some other yet to be discovered. . .'scientific creationism' is a self-contradictory, nonsense phrase. . . .Faced with these facts of evolution and the philosophical bankruptcy of their own position, creationists continually rely upon distortion and innuendo to buttress their rhetorical claim" (pp 118, 120, 123).

Or, hear Dr. Isaac Asimov's statement in the same book.

> "To those who are trained in science, creationism seems like a bad dream, a sudden reliving of a nightmare, a renewed march of an army of the night risen to challenge free thought and enlightenment. . . .Creationism, on the other hand, it not a theory. There

is no evidence, in the scientific sense, that supports it. Creationism, or at least the particular variety accepted by many Americans, is an expression of early Middle Eastern legend. It is fairly described as 'only a myth' " (pp 183, 185, 186).

Dr. Asimov, one of the foremost humanists of our day, calls the biblical account of creation "only a myth." Does that sound vaguely familiar? It certainly ought to, because Dr. Archie Manis wrote the word "myth" in the margin beside Genesis 1 in the handout that he gave to his seminar students [that document was introduced earlier in this book, and was photoreproduced for your examination]. One might come to **expect** that Asimov, an atheist, would belittle God's word and label Genesis as an "early Middle Eastern legend" or "a myth." But who in the world would ever expect a professor at Abilene Christian University to parrot those words and teach our children such concepts?! Truly, it is later than we think!

The books and handouts used by both Drs. Manis and Williams in their classes were a major portion of the discussion in the 2½-hour meeting at ACU on September 13, 1985. In fact, I **pressed** the ACU administrators who were present for a possible explanation of such documents. How, I asked, could a professor march into class and hand out to students the first page of the Bible, on which he had personally written "myth"? How, I asked, could a professor require his students to read such secularistic garbage (I know of no other words for such diatribe) and then teach it to them as factual? How, I asked, could a professor at ACU hand out to his students materials which he himself had authored [remember Dr. Manis' "Evolution Notes"?] and in which he clearly stated that evolution is a "fact" that is "rational and scientific" and "supported by an overwhelming mass of evidence"? And what answer to these questions did I receive? Naturally, I received the only reply possible under the circumstances. These items had been used, Dr. Gray contended, **as if** they were written by evolutionists **so that they could be refuted in class** by the professors!

But, when I asked for the **Scripture references** used in the biology classes to refute these items, and when I asked for the **creationist books** used in the classes to refute these items, and when I asked for the **creationist reference works** to which the students had been exposed for refutation of the evolutionary dogma, and when I asked for the **bibliography of creationist works** given to the students for their use in refuting these evolutionary concepts—all I got was a blank stare from everyone in the room. They knew—just as I knew—that there were no such items in existence, at least not from the hands of these two professors!

I cannot overemphasize this particular point, for it is, in reality, one of the major points of this book. **These materials were presented to the students in the biology classes WITHOUT ANY REFUTATION WHATSOEVER.** And if the reader doubts this statement, documentation will presently be given, **in abundance**, to substantiate it. One of the first things which led us to this conclusion was the reaction of Dr. Archie Manis, when one of his seminar students requested that he be able to hand out materials to the students in that class, published by Apologetics Press, Inc. **refuting evolution**, and presenting the scientific and biblical case for creation. Dr. Manis begrudgingly allowed the student to hand out photocopies of some of our materials, but not before he made the comment to the class (notice: to the class!) that he certainly wished that he had the class time to **refute** these "creationist materials." Question: why would a professor in ACU's biology department want to **refute** materials opposing theistic and organic evolution and presenting the biblical and scientific case for creation? Once again, the question answers itself.

But, without a doubt the most "telling" outcome of the meeting—especially when the long-range implications are considered and all the facts are in—has to do with this writer's request that each of the two professors involved in teaching evolution provide us with a statement such as outlined in the Willeford document above. And so it is now to this crucial issue that we turn our attention for the next few pages. The story that is told in this scenario is one of the most shocking revelations of the entire controversy.

As the September 13 meeting ended, I asked what **solution** ACU suggested to the problem which had been so thoroughly documented. As the Willeford document indicates, Dub Orr spoke up, confessing that the University's "aprons were not

entirely clean," but that the problem would "be corrected."
I could hardly believe my ears. For seven long months the
University officials and professors had completely ignored my
letters. For more than half a year they had perpetrated a massive cover-up of absolutely mammoth proportions. For twenty-
eight weeks I had been deceived. And, now, they wanted me
to simply "take their word" that the problem would "be corrected"?! I made it abundantly clear that such a "solution"
was merely wishful thinking on their part, and that there would
have to be tangible, empirical evidence forthcoming which
would **prove**—to everyone involved—that the professors
involved would no longer be able to propagate these destructive teachings. I subsequently insisted that **each** of the two
professors involved author and sign a statement, the contents
of which were very carefully spelled out [examine points 1-7
in the Willeford document] . In fact, the contents of the documents were **so carefully spelled out** that the ACU administrators immediately took issue with them. "Oh no," they said.
"We could **never** ask our professors to sign such statements.
Why, it would be an insult to them."

Question: how could it be an insult to ask a Christian
professor to sign a document in which he stated that he did
not believe Genesis 1-11 to be a myth, that he **did** believe
Genesis 1-11 to be literal and historical, that he did **not** believe in or advocate organic evolution or theistic evolution,
and in which he stated that he **did**, and **would**, refute such
false concepts concerning evolution. How could such be an
"insult"—unless, of course, the professors had something **to
hide**? I stood amazed—and still do to this day—at the unwil-
lingness of men of God who are professors of science in one
of "our" universities to sign such a statement.

All the disclaimers of the administrators notwithstanding, I stood firm on my request. Either the professors would
sign the statements—as specified—or the University could
attempt to explain to an inquiring brotherhood the very things
which had been quite inexplicable in this very meeting!
Apparently the University officials decided it might be better
to attempt to get the professors to sign at least **something**, than
to try to explain all of these materials to our inquisitive
brotherhood. [NOTE: It is apparent to me, now that the dead-

line for the statements to be signed has passed, that the ACU administrators never had any intention of securing the documents as specified in that meeting, but in fact, were merely attempting to "buy time" in order to try to "undo" some of the damage that had already been caused. An examination of the two professors' "documents," as reproduced below, will demonstrate the truthfulness of this assessment.]

As I prepared to leave the September 13 meeting, I made one thing crystal clear to the University officials. I was placing this "disclaimer" on the meeting: **if** the documents were not forthcoming by the date agreed upon (October 31, 1985), or **if** the documents were not **as specified** in the meeting (i.e., containing the items in points 1-7 of the Willeford document), the University could consider this meeting as **never having occurred**, and the materials **would be published** so that the brotherhood could learn firsthand of the problems herein outlined. One of the last statements I made to those present was this: "Do **not** send me some nebulous, one-or-two-sentence statement from the professors that asserts: 'we believe in God and Jesus and the Bible and creation,' for if you do, such statements will **not** be acceptable. Make certain that the statements contain the items listed, or do not even bother sending them." I then asked Dr. Ian Fair, who had been taking notes on a yellow legal-type note pad, if he had each of the items listed. He stated that he did. [NOTE: This is a most crucial point. As you will learn at a later point, Dr. Fair's notes will play a crucial part in what happens **after** the "documents" are submitted. The reader is asked to keep this in mind: there **were** notes made by the administrators as to what items were to be contained in the documents.]

I left the meeting that Friday morning, having promised those present three things. First, I pledged that I would abide by the deadline (October 31, 1985) which had been set. I would not send any packets of materials regarding this matter to anyone else prior to October 31, or the arrival of the documents, whichever came first. Second, I agreed **not** to publish a single word regarding this controversy, until after October 31, and I agreed not to publish then, if the documents were forthcoming as specified. Third, I agreed to circulate the professors' documents, upon receiving them by October 31, to every person on my mailing list to whom I had sent prior materials concerning this matter, so that the individuals and/or churches involved would know of the settlement of the controversy. I kept my word on each of these points. I left the President's conference room and went directly to my motel room. From there, I called my secretary in Montgomery and told her to pull the article (regarding this controversy) which would have been published in late September. At the same time, I gave her specific instructions that no more packets of materials on this matter were to leave our office. We kept our word. We did not publish, and we did not send out a single packet before the documents arrived.

The time frame from September 13 to October 31 was one of extreme interest to us, as it turns out. During that approximate six-week period, first one event and then another took place that was to shed additional light on the problem as it then existed. For example, consider the following.

(1) Just three days after the September 13 meeting, Dr. Archie Manis penned a letter (seven short lines long) to Mr. & Mrs. Lobley in Texline, Texas [remember, it was the Lobleys who first wrote the University over two years ago to complain because Dr. Manis had taught their daughter evolution, without any refutation, thereby causing her much confusion and some "faith problems"]. Was there any apology in Dr. Manis' letter to the Lobleys for what he had done? Absolutely not! Was there any attempted explanation for the teaching, without refutation, of evolution to their daughter? Not a word! Was there any sign of repentance forthcoming for the terrible mistake of this professor—a mistake which had caused these parents and their daughter much grief? None. The entire seven-line letter was simply "Thank you for your letter" and "God bless you and yours." Needless to say, the Lobleys were neither impressed nor satisfied. [NOTE: It will be of specific interest to the reader to learn that Dr. Manis even telephoned the Lobleys. During that telephone conversation, Dr. Manis **denied** ever teaching evolution **at all** to their daughter. Mrs. Lobley answered the phone, and Dr. Manis thought he was speaking only to her. Unbeknown to him, Mrs. Lobley's husband, Jerry, had picked up the extension phone, and heard this denial as well (two witnesses!). Later, Dr. Manis tried to

change his story, and **admitted teaching evolution—WITH-OUT REFUTATION!** Apparently Dr. Manis—and those at the University who attempt to exonerate him—can't quite get their story straight!]

(2) Oddly enough, on that same day the chairman of the biology department, Dr. John Little, penned a similar letter. [Wonder what "prompted" this sudden flurry of letters by all of these ACU folks?????] However, Dr. Little's letter was a page-and-a-half long, single-spaced. After some syrupy statements in the first part of the letter about how all his faculty members believed in God and Jesus, Dr. Little then fired a salvo at this writer. Here are his words, from the fifth paragraph of his letter to Mr. & Mrs. Lobley:

> "That brings me to the current issue of credibility with Dr. Thompson. He apparently has not been convinced that our teachers believe what they state they believe. He is currently using the testimony of a very few students (four, by his admission) who apparently misunderstood what some of the teachers were presenting. This is in contrast to hundreds who did not misunderstand. He has made some very serious accusations against his Brethren when he has no first-hand knowledge, and very limited second-hand knowledge and information."

To Dr. Little's statements, I make the following reply. He says that I apparently do not believe what his teachers say they believe. Quite the contrary: I **believe**—just as they stated in their handouts and classroom lectures—that they believe in evolution. Period! Obviously Dr. Little cannot have reference to any other statements from the professors, **because I had never received any reply of any kind from either of them, written or oral!**

Dr. Little stated that I admitted to using the testimony of only four students. I made no such admission. In fact, Dr. Little admitted to Mrs. Lobley in the very next paragraph of his letter that he **wasn't even in the meeting.** So much for **his** "credibility." I never stated or implied that I was using the testimony of only "four students." Also, doesn't it make a neat little package—all properly wrapped and tied—to simply say that the students "misunderstood"? How does one "misunderstand" when a professor states bluntly that evolution is a "fact"? How does one "misunderstand" when that same professor **writes**—across the Genesis account of creation from the very first page of the Bible itself—that Genesis is a "myth"? Ah, yes. How those poor, naive students have "misunderstood" the learned professor(s)!

Lastly, I stand amazed at Dr. Little's statements that I have "no first-hand knowledge" and only "limited second-hand knowledge." That is an amazing indictment from a man who, by his own admission, wasn't even in the meeting to see the evidences presented! Dub Orr, the member of the ACU Board of Trustees, couldn't "explain" the evidences presented. Dr. Ian Fair, Dean of the College of Biblical Studies called the materials authored by the two professors "rotten." And the best Dr. Gray, Vice-President for Academic Affairs, could do was mumble something about how the professor must have written "myth" across the Genesis account of creation so he could show the students how an evolutionist would do it! Really, now, Dr. Little! No "first-hand knowledge"? Only "limited second-hand knowledge"? Anyone with half a brain, one eye, and the ability to see through a ladder could detect that ruse! Whatever else Dr. Little may wish to say, one thing stands out clearly. Whatever "evidences" I presented in that September 13 meeting, they were weighty enough, well-documented enough, thorough enough, and serious enough to make the ACU administrators who were present acquiesce to my demands for the documents from the two professors. Doesn't that tell you something? Indeed it does! [By the way, Dr. Little sent that same letter to other parties who had written him as well. In fact, on that same day, September 16, he sent the exact same letter to Mr. and Mrs. Joe Hershey of Texline, Texas. One wonders who else received this "pearl of wisdom" from Dr. Little?]

(3) Now Dr. Kenneth Williams enters the picture. It would have been better for him had he not. On October 1, Dr. Williams wrote a letter to Mr. & Mrs. Hershey, of Texline, Texas, in response to a serious letter they had written him, asking for an explanation of why he was teaching evolution in his classes.

Dr. Williams responded in part by stating emphatically to the Hersheys that "In my 18 years of teaching here at Abilene Christian University, you are the first persons to question what I am teaching other than Mr. Bert Thompson and Mr. Mark Scott." That may be what Dr. Williams **wishes** were true, but I can assure you that it is not what **is** true! Consider this, if you will. [And as you read, be alert to the evidence which is about to be presented regarding how **long** the teaching of evolution—raw evolution—has been going on at ACU!]

As the reader recalls from the Willeford document, in presenting some "background" material on myself to those at the September 13 meeting (at their request) I mentioned that I travel almost every weekend, speaking across the length and breadth of our country, **against** evolution and **for** the Genesis account of creation. As odd as it may seem (providence??), it was in those travels that I discovered how untruthful Dr. Williams had been when he attempted to portray himself to the Hersheys as never having been accused of teaching evolution over the past many (18) years. One of the places I spoke shortly after the September 13 meeting was at the Park Church of Christ in Oskaloosa, Iowa. The congregation is a small, "mission" church of approximately 50 members. Two evangelists, supported by other churches, labor with the Park Church of Christ. One of those ministers is Dale Burleson. Dale holds a B.S. degree in biology from (you guessed it) Abilene Christian University. He also holds an M.S. degree in wildlife and fisheries science from Texas A&M University. So, since he and I have **two** alma maters in common, it would not be unusual for us to discuss those institutions during my visit to Oskaloosa. And discuss we did. During our conversation (who would have guessed that I would have stumbled across such valuable information on a weekend speaking engagement in Oskaloosa, Iowa?), I asked Dale the following question. "You graduated only a year or two after I did from ACU. Were you ever taught organic or theistic evolution in any of your biology classes at ACU, **without refutation?**" I don't think I'll ever forget the look on Dale's face, or the answer he gave to my question. He leaned back in his chair (we were sitting in his living room at the time, awaiting the evening meal), looked me straight in the face, and said, "Was I?! You'd better believe I was!" Then Dale went on to tell me the story which, no doubt, Dr. Kenneth Williams wishes were forgotten. Dale told me how he enrolled in a biology seminar class taught by Dr. Williams in the spring of 1972 (ACU's course number was Bio 4196), and that Dr. Williams presented evolution and only evolution, and **that** as **fact**. I asked Dale if there was any refutation of it presented in class. He said, "Absolutely not!" But that was not all that Dale Burleson said. He went on to point out that he, personally, considered Dr. Williams' teaching "dangerous" (that was his exact phrase). In fact, he said, he considered it **so dangerous** that once he was outside the University environs, **after** his graduation (where his grades couldn't be tampered with??), he wrote a lengthy letter to the biology department, complaining about the teaching of evolution, **without any refutation**. I asked him if he received a reply, so that he would know that his letter had, in fact, been received. Guess what? He **did**! Now, what was that, Dr. Williams, about no one challenging your teaching of evolution in all of the 18 years that you've been at ACU? Not so!

However, as important as that information is, there is an additional "pearl of great price" to be found in this little episode. That "pearl" is this. It was in **1972** that Dale Burleson took Dr. Kenneth Williams for the seminar course. Guess what book was **required reading**? What book did Williams **require** the students to purchase as the **textbook for the course**? [See if this sounds familiar??] The textbook for the course was, *Evolution, Genetics, and Man*, authored by prominent evolutionary geneticist of The Rockefeller University, Dr. Theodosius Dobzhansky! As we talked in Dale's living room, he got up, walked into his study, and literally pulled the book from the shelf. He still had it in his personal library! Need I tell you the tone of the book? The book (and I might add, it was certainly no stranger to me) is literally filled with page after page after page of the "proofs" of organic evolution. This comes as no great shock. Those of us who work in the creation/evolution field know Dr. Dobzhansky quite well. He is the evolutionist who is famous not only for work in the field of genetics, but for his now-classic statement which is so often quoted: "Nothing in biology makes sense except in the light of evolution." Though he is now deceased (he died in 1975), he was very much alive in 1972. And his book, *Evolution, Genetics, and Man* (published by John Wiley & Sons of New York) became a classic in the field of evolutionary genetics.

Perhaps the reader would be interested in a quotation or two from the book, which was **mandated** for use **in 1972** by seminar students in biology. Consider, if you will, the following.

(1) "Biological evolution is a part of the evolution of the cosmos. The rise and development of mankind are a part of the story of biological evolution. **Man cannot reach a valid understanding of his own nature without a knowledge of his own biological background**. It may, then, be that **the study of evolutionary biology is the most important practical endeavor open to the human mind**. Accordingly, an effort is being made in this book to show to the student that biology is not only a craft which is interesting to technicians and devotees **but also a part of the fabric of modern humanistic thought**" (p vii, emphasis added).

(2) "Man is a biological species, subject to the action of biological forces, and **a product of a long evolutionary development. . .the evidence shows conclusively that man arose from forebears who were not men. . . .**For similar reasons, it is not a matter of personal taste whether or not we 'believe in' evolution. **The evidence for evolution is compelling**. Moreover, human evolution is going on at present, and, what is more, biology is in the process of acquiring knowledge which may permit man to control and direct this evolution" (pp 319, 320, emphasis added).

(3) "**Biology gives no warrant for the belief that man was preformed in the primordial life, or that the evolution of life as a whole had as its purpose the production of man**. Evolution does not strive to accomplish any particular purpose or to reach any specific goal except the preser-

vation of life itself. **Evolution did not happen according to a predetermined plan.** Nevertheless, when man contemplates the whole perspective of the evolution of the Cosmos, he can see that **the origin of mankind was one of the outstanding events in the history of creation by evolution**" (p 374, emphasis added).

(4) "...man could not have arisen directly from mud, since as a child he is unable to feed or to take care of himself. Hence **he must have arisen from another animal.** This, then, is the first statement of the view that man is biologically unique. At present we are confident that **man is a product of biological evolution**; his evolution was brought about by the same fundamental causes as the evolution of all other organisms" (pp 3, 4 emphasis added).

And just think: all of this has been going on since **at least** 1972 (and possibly prior to that since Williams has taught for 18 years!) on the campus of Abilene Christian University. Yet we are being told, "Why, you are the very first to ever call us into question regarding our teachings." Nothing could be farther from the truth! And, of course, one can only wonder how many more such students there are "out there" somewhere who have similar stories to tell. How many more are there—whose names we shall likely never know—who were taught evolution by these professors at a **Christian** university?

(4) Now it is time for the President of the University to have his say in these matters. On October 8, Dr. Bill Teague, President of Abilene Christian University, penned a three-paragraph letter to Mrs. F.W. Carruth, of Texline, Texas. Dr. Teague's letter was in response to a letter written by Mrs. Carruth, complaining about the teaching of evolution in biology classes at the University. Now, as you read Dr. Teague's letter (reproduced below), keep in mind that this is approximately three weeks **after** my September 13 meeting with the ACU administrators. Notice how Dr. Teague handles Mrs. Carruth's complaints—all the while in possession of the knowledge that the two documents from the two professors had

been agreed to by the University, and were, in fact, due on my desk in only 23 days. With that in mind, examine Dr. Teague's statements and see if they represent an honest appraisal of the situation as it then stood.

"Dear Mrs. Carruth:

Thank you for your interest in the teaching program at Abilene Christian University. After a full investigation in which representatives of our Board of Trustees have participated, I am able to state that the Genesis account of Creation is the only account of Creation that is advocated by our faculty. These men and women openly affirm their faith in God and in the scriptures. Many serve effectively in leadership positions in local congregations. These good people have been treated unfairly by the unsubstantiated statements of one or two students who take classroom notes and materials out of context and sequence in their allegation of impropriety. It is unfortunate that this kind of misleading information has been disseminated. Representatives from the administration of ACU are available to meet with you to have a full discussion of the matter, should that be necessary to clear up any misunderstanding.
                    Sincerely yours, William J. Teague."

Were it not so serious, the Teague letter would almost be laughable. Notice, first, that "representatives" of the Board of Trustees were **not** present in the September 13 meeting. A lone, single "representative"—Dub Orr—was present. Notice, second, that in his leading Mrs. Carruth to believe that a "full investigation" had taken place, he quite conveniently omitted the fact that the evidences presented had not been anywhere near explained, and that the two professors involved were, in fact, having to produce statements which corrected the errors they had been teaching for many, many years. Why was there no mention by Dr. Teague of these facts? Notice also that the materials are dubbed as "unsubstantiated" and that they are taken "out of context." How "unsubstantiated" can something be when it comes directly from the hands of the professors themselves? **They** wrote the handouts. **They** (Manis) called the Genesis account of creation a **myth. They** taught evolution as a fact. How much **more** substantiation does one need? And about that claim that the materials were "taken out of context"? First, let us note that every false teacher with whom we have ever dealt tried to "weasle out" of his error by stating that he had been quoted "out of context." Second, let us ask this penetrating question: in what context **could** a professor write "myth" across the Genesis account of creation and be correct? In what context could a **Christian** university professor walk into a classroom of impressionable young freshmen and state that he is "an elder in the church" and that he "believes in evolution" and that the students "will learn it and believe in it too"? In what context do such things become right? We would like an answer to that question.

Of course, President Teague's hesitancy to accept the evidence—**any** evidence—comes as no surprise. For, you see, on August 19, 1985 he wrote a letter to Mr. and Mrs. Ned Martin of Rockwall, Texas. Mr. and Mrs. Martin had, like Mrs. Carruth, written to complain about the teaching of evolution in the biology department at ACU. In his August 19 letter, Dr. Teague stated specifically, "Please send me as soon as possible a copy of the documents you mentioned in your correspondence so an appropriate action may be taken." The documents **were** sent to Dr. Teague. How do we know? We know because **we** provided the documents for Mr. & Mrs. Martin. And they were the same exact documents which were used in the September 13 meeting. But did Dr. Teague "act on" these documents? Did he "correct" the situation in any way? Did he "discipline" these erring professors? Did he chastise the department head in biology who had allowed these false teachings to go on for so long? Of course, the answer to each of these questions is a resounding "NO!" Instead, Dr. Teague simply "looked the other way," ordered a continued cover-up, and began writing letters claiming that these poor, pitiful, mistreated faculty members had been maligned and "misunderstood." How can these things be? And at a **Christian** university!

(5) Amidst all of this, it is at least refreshing to know that there are **some** who are not swayed by "smooth and fair speech" such as that offered by President Teague. One who was not was Mr. Grady Lobley of Midland, Texas. On the same day (October 8) that Dr. Teague wrote Mrs. Carruth, he sent the same exact letter to Mr. Lobley, who had written him earlier to complain about the teaching of evolution in the biology classes at ACU. Dr. Teague's letter about how "good people" had been treated "unfairly" didn't "ring true" with Mr. Lobley for several reasons, not the least of which was that he had seen, firsthand, the evidences from the two professors' classes. On October 14, 1985 Mr. Lobley wrote a lengthy letter to Dr. Teague. A portion of that letter is reproduced below:

> "The 'full investigation' which you mentioned was attended by how many people? Were Williams and Manis present? I believe that the only account of Creation being taught is the Genesis Account, **if** one qualifies your statement. I have geologist friends who think that the Genesis account of Creation and the theory of organic evolution are compatible. This leaves one free to believe the organic evolution theory. Is this not what Manis and Williams believe? They do, in fact, believe and teach organic evolution theory, do they not? And somehow still believe the Genesis account? We were concerned about this teaching about two years ago, I believe. I doubt that these 'good people' have been treated unfairly by unsubstantiated statements. Let us hope that the truth will surface. Will ACU now try to ridicule or discredit students who have had their faith disturbed by these men? It is preposterous to think that faith has been disturbed by teachers at a Christian school! Faith supposedly is strengthened there! A student taking a course may fear reprisal if he speaks up against a professor's teaching. Does ACU fear a loss of standing in the academic community if it does not teach the 'theory'? A Christian school can be The Church's strongest helper or can become its

greatest liability. Why teach evolution at all? The students have heard the theory from early years. Have certain teachers at ACU required students to sign teacher evaluation forms? Why?

Sincerely yours,
(signed) Grady D. Lobley"

Mr. Lobley does indeed raise some interesting points. It **is** preposterous that a student's faith should be "disturbed" at a **Christian** school. And is it just possible that ACU fears it **will** lose its standing in the academic community if it does not propagate the teaching of evolution as factual? And of course, from Mark Scott's experience with Dr. Manis, we already **know** that a student **may** suffer a "reprisal" if he speaks up against the teaching of a certain professor. Apparently Dr. Teague's letters are not falling on the sympathetic ears he thought they would. Rightly so!

By this time in the controversy, one month had passed since the September 13 meeting that took place on the campus of ACU. And still, we had heard not a word from anyone. Of course, there were still eighteen days remaining until October 31, and so we were determined to wait, as we promised we would. However, on October 13 I did pen a letter to Dr. C.G. Gray, Vice-President for Academic Affairs, **reminding** him of the fact that those present in the September 13 meeting had given their word as Christians that the documents, as specified, would be forthcoming. The text of my letter to Dr. Gray is reproduced below.

"Dear Dr. Gray:

"I send you greetings from those of us associated with the work of Apologetics Press, and hope that this letter finds you well.

"As you may remember, on Friday morning, September 13th, I met with you and other representatives of the ACU Administration and/or Board, regarding the charges that have been made against some of your biology professors concerning their teaching (to be accepted as true) evolution to students in their classes. During the meeting I presented evidence to substantiate my claim that indeed, these two professors (Drs. Archie Manis and Kenneth Williams) **were** teaching evolution as factual. The evidence, though not accepted *in toto* by you, remained unexplained. Subsequently, I asked for statements from the two professors involved, stating: (A) that they did not believe Genesis 1-11 to be a myth; (B) that they would not teach organic evolution, theistic evolution, or any forms of them, to students as factual; (C) that they do accept Genesis 1-11 as literal and historical and will teach them as such; (D) that they will not teach organic evolution or theistic evolution in their classes, except to refute them, and; (E) that they repent of having taught evolution to students in the past without making it clear that it was false and not to be accepted.

"Those men present in the meeting gave me their word as Christians that the statements from the two professors would be on my desk no later than October 31, 1985. It has now been one month to the day since my meeting with you, and still I have neither received the documents nor heard from you by letter or by phone. Consequently, I am penning this letter, merely as a reminder of the fact that you promised to have the documents, containing the items as listed above, on my desk by October 31. That is now just eighteen days away. As I mentioned in my meeting with you, I will expect the documents, as specified, in my office by that time or the materials which I presented that day, plus additional materials which have since come into my possession, will be made public and the brotherhood at-large will then be the judge of these matters. I have kept my word to you that I would: (A) refrain from publicizing this material in any form, and; (B) refrain from publishing any materials relating to this matter, until after October 31, 1985. I certainly hope that those of you at ACU fully intend to keep your word as Christians as well. I will anxiously await the arrival of the documents from the two professors.

Sincerely,
(signed) Bert Thompson, Ph.D."

On October 23, 1985 Dr. Gray penned a two-paragraph letter to this writer. Enclosed with the letter were two "statements," one each from Kenneth Williams and Archie Manis.

Dr. Gray's letter, and the content of the two "documents" from the two professors, bear examination. Dr. Gray's letter stated:

> "Dear Dr. Thompson:
>
> "Enclosed are the statements from Dr. Williams and Dr. Manis. These statements are for your information and should not be duplicated for distribution. Your letter of October 13 indicates several areas that need further discussion. I will be happy to discuss these with you by telephone or meet with you; or you may prefer to contact Mr. Orr, Dr. Fair, or Dr. Reeves.
>
> Sincerely,
> (signed) C.G. Gray"

Now, before presenting the "documents" from the two professors, a comment or two regarding Dr. Gray's cover letter is appropriate. First, notice that Dr. Gray **admits** in his letter that the documents are not what was agreed upon when he states that "several areas need further discussion." In fact, **nothing** needed further discussion—at least as things stood when we all left the September 13 meeting. Everyone present knew **exactly** what the documents were supposed to contain. Dr. Fair, you recall, had written down those very items. Second, notice that Dr. Gray makes a feeble attempt to keep the documents from being circulated by stating that they are for "your information and should not be duplicated for distribution." He has, of course, no right to make such a statement. I **specifically** told those present in the September 13 meeting that one of the purposes in asking for the statements from the two professors was so that they **could** be circulated. In fact, one is forced to ask, if the documents were correct, and contained the items specified in the September 13 meeting, why would Dr. Gray (and the two professors) **not** want them circulated?! By stating that the documents were **not** to be circulated, Dr. Gray has (inadvertently, no doubt) brought considerable suspicion upon the credibility both of the documents and the two professors involved. We repeat: if the documents, as sent by Dr.

Gray and as written by the two professors, **were** presented **as requested**, why restrict their circulation? **If** they were correct, their circulation would be of utmost value in stopping the rapidly spreading information (deemed by ACU to be false) concerning the teaching of evolution on campus!

Now examine the professors' "statements." But before you do, be sure to go back and read (pp 83,84) from the Willeford summary of the September 13 meeting exactly what **should have been** in the documents, **as agreed upon** by those in attendance. Also, remember my disclaimer, as presented at the end of the meeting, about what the University could expect if they sent a one or two sentence general statement. Then, examine the statements as presented below. The first is from Dr. Kenneth Williams. It came in the form of a letter addressed to Dr. C.G. Gray. It stated:

> "Dear Dr. Gray:
>
> "Let me state unequivocally that I believe in the Bible, in Christianity, and in the biblical account of creation as recorded in Genesis, and I do not advocate organic evolution.
>
> Sincerely yours,
(signed) Kenneth B. Williams, Ph.D."

The second statement was from Dr. Archie Manis. It was addressed as simply "TO WHOM IT MAY CONCERN" and contained, in numbered points, the following items:

> "1. I believe in God, the God of the Holy Bible.
>
> "2. I believe the Holy Bible is God's inspired word.
>
> "3. I believe in the Genesis account of creation.
>
> "4. I have believed in all of the above since I was about eleven.
>
> "5. I do not advocate organic evolution, and I never have.
>
> "6. 'Evolution Notes,' a four-page handout for my seminar students in the spring of 1985, is simply my summary of many different readings

in evolution theory. It was intended exclusively for my students, for their reference use; it was not used as a basis of discussion; it was designed to inform those who were quite ignorant of basic evolutionary theory.

Signed this 9th day of October, 1985: Archie L. Manis, Ph.D. One of the elders of the Baker Heights Church of Christ, Abilene, Texas."

These statements from the two professors are the total content of the two documents. Remember the "disclaimer" I put on the September 13 meeting? Do not send a one or two sentence statement about "I believe in God and the Bible and Jesus." Then what does the University send from Dr. Williams? A one-sentence statement which says just that!! Then Archie Manis takes six points to say exactly the same. But, in Dr. Manis' statement there are several items of interest. However, before we examine those, note what the two professors' statements do **not** state: (1) They do **not** say one word about whether or not they believe, and have taught, **theistic** evolution, progressive creation, mitigated evolution, etc.; (2) They do **not** state in their documents that they have refuted, and will continue to refute, organic evolution, theistic evolution, etc.; (3) They do **not** state that Genesis 1-11 is not myth; (4) They do **not** contend that they believe Genesis 1-11 is a **literal, historical** account of God's creative activity; (5) They do **not** repent of having taught evolution and/or theistic evolution in such a way as to leave the impression with their students that these false concepts may be accepted by a faithful child of God.

In other words, the statements do not remotely conform to the items specifically agreed upon in the September 13 meeting as necessary elements of the documents. But look again at Dr. Manis' statement. Notice that Dr. Manis states that he does not advocate organic evolution, and never has. What, then, of the statements of **witnesses** like Brenda Lobley, Mark Scott, and others? Does their testimony count for nothing simply because they are "just students"? If you are inclined to believe that it does count for nothing, then you will find the next section of this booklet extremely interesting, because in that section evidence will be presented (some of it in Dr. Manis' own handwriting) which will establish, beyond the shadow of a doubt, that he has, and does, advocate organic evolution. But notice the statement in point number 6 of Dr. Manis' statement which literally leaps off the page at you as you read it. Remember, if you will, that the **only** explanation offered in the September 13 meeting regarding Dr. Manis' class handouts was that he wrote them "as if an evolutionist had written them, so that they could be [are you ready for this?] **discussed** and **refuted in class**." Now look at the totally contradictory, and self-incriminating statement made by Dr. Manis himself. He says, concerning those very handouts which caused this furor in the first place: " 'Evolution Notes,' a four-page handout for my seminar students in the spring of 1985, is simply my summary of many different readings in evolution theory. . .**it was not used as a basis of discussion**." Now, which are we to believe? Dr. Gray, and the other ACU administrators present in the September 13 meeting told us that the documents were written for the specific purpose of being "discussed in class, and refuted." **Now, Dr. Manis himself concedes that the documents were "not used as a basis of discussion."** Honestly, do these people from ACU think that brethren are **that stupid**? Well, they are not! When one side says the handouts were presented to be discussed and refuted, and the other side says that they were **never** discussed, it is pretty obvious that the folks haven't even bothered to take time to get their stories together. As to the claim from Dr. Gray that the handouts were "refuted"—let us simply say that it is hardly possible to "refute" something that was never even **discussed**!!

Perhaps now the reader can see what Wayne Jackson meant in his introduction to this volume when he suggested that the materials are, in many instances, "incredible and unbelievable." I think I would be hard-pressed to state it any better!

It is, quite honestly, beyond my comprehension that ACU could forward to us these two "documents" (and we use that word loosely) and expect us to accept them as even vaguely resembling what was agreed upon in the September 13 meeting. Once we had received the two professors' "statements," it was clear to us that the ACU administrators had no intention of sending us the documents, as specified in the meeting. That being the case, we penned one last letter to Dr. Gray. That letter is reproduced below.

"November 1, 1985

"Dear Dr. Gray:

"We are in receipt of your letter of October 23, and the two 'documents' from Professors Manis and Williams.

"You, of course, fully realize (and your cover letter indicates that you realize) that these documents from Professors Manis and Williams do not even **remotely** conform to what we **all** agreed on in our meeting in the President's Conference Room at Abilene Christian University on the morning of September 13, 1985.

"This is extremely regrettable, especially in light of the fact that you **gave me your word as a Christian** that the documents, **as outlined in the meeting**, would be forthcoming by no later than October 31, 1985. It is clear, from the content of the documents, that you are not a man of your word. Apparently you had, from the very beginning, no intention of keeping your promise(s).

"This being the case, further discussion would be futile.

Sincerely,
(signed) Bert Thompson, Ph.D.''

⌐═══✕✕✕═══┐

4

An Avalanche of Evidence

Mrs. L.D. Swift: *"Archie,...do you refute the teaching of evolution as it is presented in the books you use?"*

Archie Manis: *"No! I never do."*

Mrs. L.D. Swift: *"Archie, I don't understand that. Why don't you?"*

Archie Manis: *"...I deal only with the material in the book just as it is presented and nothing less, except supplementary notes which I give out at times. But these notes do not refute evolution. The biology classroom is no place to refute evolution."*

(Conversation on October 28, 1985 between Mrs. L.D. Swift and Dr. Archie Manis regarding Dr. Manis' teaching of evolution at ACU. Recorded in Swift document of November 2, 1985, pp 4.6–4.8.)

"Evolution is a fact, not a theory. It once was a theory, but today, as a consequence of observation and testing it is probably the best authenticated actuality known to science. There are theories concerning mechanisms of evolution, but

no competent student doubts the reality of evolution."

—Dr. Ashley Montagu
Famed humanist/evolutionist in book
he edited, **Science and Creationism**;
text required by Dr. Archie Manis in his
spring, 1985 ACU biology seminar class

Since November 1, 1985 we have been gathering additional evidence regarding these matters, and at the same time working on the text of this booklet. We never hid our intentions from those at ACU who were involved in this matter. From the very beginning we made it clear that **if** the matter was not corrected, the evidences would be made public. We have kept our word at every step of the way. University officials have refused to take appropriate corrective action. The only alternative open to those who are unwilling to sit idly by and allow their children to be openly and boldy taught evolution, without **any** refutation, is to make known to the brotherhood at-large the ongoings of the past eleven months, in hopes that those in the churches of Christ will not allow such to continue. Though the University has continually expressed through its actions a "don't care" attitude that suggests "we do not have to answer to you, or anyone else," it is our sincere hope that those responsible for such an attitude will soon learn that the University does, in fact, have to answer to those who have made it what it is today.

From the very beginning of this controversy—as far back as February, 1985—the evidences which arrested our attention have been quite literally incontrovertible. Those evidences have ranged from the word "myth" written on the Genesis account of creation in one of the professors' own handwriting, to handouts authored by one of the professors in which evolution is openly and unashamedly called a "fact" of science that is "rational and logical." And with every passing day, the **amount** of evidence has grown until it finally reached a point that even **we** thought that there simply could not be anything **more** damaging than what we had already seen and heard. But we were wrong.

Some of the evidence which we originally possessed was in our hands because it was purposely sent to us by students or parents who were concerned about what was happening at this **Christian** university. Additional material came into our possession because of intensive, time-consuming research on our part—research that covered several months and that included a dogged determination to get to the bottom of this most serious matter. Still other evidence appeared, quite unsolicited, and simply "fell into our lap" as it were—from sources heretofore unknown to us. But as the months rolled by, one thing became crystal clear: **the massive amount of evidence simply could not be ignored**.

Then, suddenly, a document arrived at our doorstep quite unannounced. And though it appeared quietly, the impact it was to have would belie its unassuming entrance. A word of explanation is in order.

During this months-long investigation, news of the fiasco in the biology department on the ACU campus spread far and wide. Individuals heard about it, elderships got the word, entire congregations became informed. And little wonder! The report of evolution being taught in one of "our" schools is not the kind of news that can be easily stifled (though the ACU administration has given it their best shot). First one person, and then multiplied others, began to hear about the controversy. As news of what was happening began to spread, mail began to pour into our office. Our phones rang day and night. People—interested brethren—wanted to know. **How** can this be happening? And what can we do about it? We received letters of commendation from young and old, well-educated and uneducated, educators and laborers alike. Each letter expressed **gratitude** that something was being done, and **hope** that as a final result the teaching of evolution would no longer be tolerated on the campus of a Christian university. Letters of encouragement arrived from the editors of many of our brotherhood's best-known, and most widely-respected journals. Letters came from students. Letters came from parents and grandparents; from aunts and uncles. Letters came from friends of families. And then, one day, the letter arrived from Mr. and Mrs. L.D. Swift of Tuscola, Texas, near Abilene.

Mr. and Mrs. Swift have been faithful members of the

church for many years. He is an electrical engineer and graduate of the Bear Valley School of Preaching; she is a high school teacher. In fact, for some years they worshipped in Abilene at the Baker Heights Church of Christ—the congregation where Dr. Archie Manis now serves as an elder. It was about those times at the Baker Heights congregation, and specifically about Archie Manis, that the Swifts wrote. The story they told is sad, but so pertinent to this investigation.

Brother and sister Swift wrote because they had heard, through various sources in Abilene, about the controversy over Archie Manis' teaching of evolution in his biology classes at ACU. But it was not their letter which made their story so vital to this investigation. It was the **document** that accompanied their letter. Appended to their letter was a document 33 pages in length. It was entitled, "Statement of Witness Concerning Dr. Archie Manis, Professor of Biology at ACU and Elder at the Baker Heights Church of Christ in Abilene, Texas." The story told in the document is one that is utterly incredible! Unfortunately, the entire document cannot be duplicated here because of its length. However, major portions of it **are** reproduced below, with the full permission of both Mr. and Mrs. Swift. The document is dated November 2, 1985 and was presented not only to this writer, but also to the individual elders of the Baker Heights Church of Christ and to certain ACU administrators.

Here, in capsulized form, is the story. One evening in 1981, while the Swifts were members of the Baker Heights congregation, they attended a regular meeting of a church visitation group. This meeting was held in Archie Manis' home. During the course of the evening, the topic of evolution came up for discussion. The Swift's document stated:

"The topic of discussion which is reported here concerns the subject of evolution, especially the origin of man and Genesis 1. Archie explained his approach to the subject and was quizzed by my wife and me. Archie Manis was the central speaker in this discussion explaining his views on the subject of evolution and his method of relating it to his classes at ACU. My wife and I were shocked by certain statements

Archie made concerning his views of the evolution of man. This view is commonly known as 'theistic evolution.' He made it very clear that he believed that God began the creation process in some fashion which he did not explain in detail and that man has evolved from primative (sic) forms of life over great periods of time. Archie stated emphatically that the evolution of man and the animals was a proven scientific fact and indisputable. It is my clear understanding that Archie Manis does believe in the evolution of man and therefore rejects the biblical creation account of Genesis 1 and 2 as we understand it. I say this without malicious intent toward Archie, knowing that I shall stand before God some day and answer for my words and deeds. The issues concerned here are not matters of opinion or expediency. Theistic evolution relegates man to the level of a mere brute and makes God's Word a lie. It is a very serious charge we bring, but a very serious matter involved. Archie Manis is an elder at [the] Baker Heights Church of Christ. It is therefore only proper that any accusation be made by at least two witnesses. My wife and I are both witnesses of the discussion described herein. Archie made it very clear throughout the course of our discussion that he was a 'theistic evolutionist' and related his convictions in the classroom at ACU. At one point Archie stated that his students were prepared in the doctrine of evolution better than any others in the state colleges of Texas. **We asked Archie if he also presented material that refuted this theory in his classroom. He said that he did not.** We also asked Archie if he believed that the days of Genesis 1 were literal 24-hour days. He indicated that he did not believe they were but that they were probably long periods of time and corresponded with the geologic ages of modern science. As the reader may well imagine it is impossible at this point in time to recall many statements that were made with a high degree of accuracy. It was, however, very clear to us then and now that Archie made five points:

(1) He indicated that he was proud of the way he presented evolution in his classes withoutbiblicalrefutation and that he was convinced it was good and would continue in the same manner in the future.

(2) He also indicated that he was a theistic evolutionist and that he felt there was no conflict with that and the Genesis account of creation.

(3) He very clearly indicated that he doubted the days of Genesis 1 were literal 24-hour days and that he believed that the Genesis record allowed for very long periods of time as proposed by modern science.

(4) Archie did indicate that he believed that God somehow had a hand in the beginning of life on earth.

(5) He also indicated that he believed that Genesis 1 and 2 could not really be understood in the traditional way and that these chapters contained words and phrases which could be interpreted in several ways" (Swift Document, pp 3.1-3.3, emphasis added).

As a result of that discussion between the Swifts and Archie Manis, the Swifts left the Baker Heights Church of Christ and began worshipping with another area congregation. To quote the Swifts:

"My wife and I were very shocked by the position that Archie took in the discussion. As we thought on this we became incensed that a man of his position in the Church and at the college would believe such an ungodly doctrine. We wanted desperately to tell someone of authority. We discussed going to the elders at Baker Heights, but as I personally pondered this action I could not imagine how they did not already know of Archie's position and belief. How could so many people—elders, deacons, teachers, preachers, students at ACU, ACU faculty and administrators—how could all these people not know? Many had known Archie for years more than I. How could I know and they didn't? Unfortunately I concluded (I believe incorrectly now) that these people did know but did not care. I felt very much alone and frustrated beyond words. We left the fellowship of Baker Heights several months later for this reason primarily. To the best of my recollection we told only Johnny and Shirley Jennings [one of the deacons of the Baker Heights congregation—BT] and Gene Hagedorn (now deceased) about this incident. I regret our actions in this matter. I wish we had gone to the elders, but we did not" (p 7.3).

Upon learning of the **recent** controversy over the teaching of evolution by Archie Manis in his ACU biology classes, the Swifts decided that the best thing to do was to go to Archie **directly**. And so on October 28, 1985 the Swifts called Archie Manis and spoke with him for approximately one hour and thirty minutes. After a few brief words of introduction, the Swifts stated that they wanted to ask Archie Manis several questions, to which he agreed. The first question centered around the meeting in the Manis' home in 1981. But, to the Swifts' dismay, Dr. Manis said that he did not remember the meeting at all. The Swifts find that difficult to believe. Here is their explanation as to why:

"It is beyond my understanding how Archie could have forgotten a discussion of this type with people he knew and a discussion which at times became somewhat heated as emotions came to the surface in words and facial expressions. There were many pointed questions asked Archie during that discussion. His answers to these clearly indicated that Archie believed in theistic evolution as defined at the beginning of this document. What Archie really believes now cannot easily be determined with certainty because his answers are evasive in nature and filled with ambiguous terms. This is certainly not the mark of an honest man. I am personally convinced that Archie believes in theistic evolution and has little regard for the creation doctrine" (pp 7.2, 7.3).

Why would the Swifts make such a statement? On what grounds could they? The answer, it seems, lies in the telephone conversation that evening of October 28 with Dr. Manis. Consider, for example, the following part of that telephone conversation.

"L.D.: Archie, do you believe that God created heaven and earth and all things therein in six literal 24-hour days?"

"Archie: I think God could have made all things in six days. Don't you? God can do what He wants, you know."

"L.D.: Archie, we're not concerned right now with what God could have done or what He can do. We're concerned with what God said He did. Now, I'll state the question again. Do you believe the days of creation were literal 24-hour days?"

"Archie: There is a real problem with that because the sun was not made until the fourth day. How do you explain that?"

"L.D.: But Archie, doesn't Exodus 20:11 clearly indicate that the creation days were literal 24-hour days?"

"Archie: No, how can there be a 24-hour day without sun? Time cannot be measured without sun" (p 4.5)

This part of the conversation, however, was not the only evidence available to the Swifts. For, you see, the Swifts also questioned Dr. Manis regarding his teaching of evolution at ACU. Mrs. Swift (Dana) and her husband wanted to know exactly what Dr. Manis **did** teach his students.

"Dana: Archie, let me ask you a question."

"Archie: Go right ahead, Dana."

"Dana: Archie, how do you present the material in the biology classes? Do you refute the teachings of evolution as it is presented in the books you use?"

"Archie: **No! I never do.**"

"Dana: Archie, I don't understand that. Why don't you?"

"Archie: Dana, you must understand—there are several reasons."

"The following are reasons which Archie gave although they are not necessarily in the sequence which he presented them.

"(1) There is very little time in most classes to refute the materials presented in the biology textbooks. I deal only with the material in the book just as it is presented and nothing less except supplementary notes which I give out at times. **But these notes do not refute evolution.**

"(2) The biology classroom is no place to refute evolution. That should be done in the Bible class. I'd love to be teaching Bible, we all would, but I'm trained in biology so that's what I teach.

"(3) Another reason I don't refute evolution is because I assume that the students have already had that before they come to college. And also they get that kind of teaching in the Bible Department at the college.

"Dana: I cannot believe that in a Christian college, as a Christian teacher that you would not refute evolution in **any** way because even in my high school history classes I touch on evolution in a 'social' sense and I teach against the theory of evolution. I don't assume that my high school students know anything about it and I don't understand how you can 'assume' that college freshmen would know anything about how to refute evolution. . . .Do you mean to tell me that you teach these young people all these things and never refute them? Archie, how do you expect these students to be able to discern what's wrong with these theories by themselves? What about questions concerning creation from Genesis? Don't you answer their questions about creation?"

"Archie: I never get any questions like that in class, Dana."

"Dana: Now that's hard to believe! You mean to tell me that none of the students ever ask questions about creation and how it may conflict with evolution? Surely there are some with questions?"

"Archie: Well, I have very few questions like that. Maybe there's been one or two in all the years I've been teaching. You know, we get a few questions like that but not many."

"L.D.: Archie, let me go back to our discussion a bit earlier. Archie, it really concerns me that you do not ever refute evolution in your classes. That really bothers me."

"Archie: It's like I said earlier, I'm a scientist. I teach in the science department at ACU, so I teach science and not religion. Religion is taught in the Bible Department."

"L.D.:   Is that the policy of ACU?"

"Archie: Yes, but we're (we teachers) given a lot of freedom in this regard. I teach the way I want to" (pp 4.6-4.8, all emphasis added except the word "any" in Mrs. Swift's statement which begins, "I cannot believe. . .").

So there you have it. Does Dr. Manis accept the biblical creation account? Hardly! He has plainly admitted that the creation days are **not** 24-hour periods of time. And he has plainly admitted that he **does** teach evolution in his classes **without any refutation whatsoever.** He further seems to think that "someone else" (the ACU Bible department???) should refute the evolutionary concepts he presents because he is, after all, a trained scientist. Well, I beg to differ! This writer happens to also be a "trained scientist" **and** a professor at a Christian school. Yet each and every time I teach on the subject of evolution, you may rest assured that the students under my direction leave the class knowing full well that it is a godless, atheistic, humanistic system of origins that is squarely at-odds with biblical revelation, and is **not** to be accepted. Why—oh why—cannot Dr. Manis make that same statement?! Could it just possibly be because he doesn't believe evolution to be wrong?! But let me revert for a moment to point (2) above. "The biology class," asserts Manis, "is no place to refute evolution." My question is this: Is the biology class the place to **refute biblical creationism**?? Apparently Manis thinks so for that clearly is his design as indicated by: (a) his use of the book, *Science and Creationism.* (b) his handout "Research in Genesis." (c) his "Evolution Notes" [Cf.: #16] which address creationism in a very condescending way. (d) his handout, "Creationist Arguments," from Futuyma's book, *Science On Trial.* (e) his handout from Kitcher's book, *Abusing Science: The Case Against Creationism.* If one is strictly committed to the teaching of biological science, what purpose on earth does the inclusion of these materials serve?! One would have to be totally blind not to see what Dr. Manis is attempting to do.

In my meeting with ACU administrators on September 13, the **only** possible explanation offered for the professors' handouts teaching evolution as fact was that these handouts were given to the students **to be refuted**! Now, along comes Manis boasting—from his own mouth in front of two witnesses—that he has **never** refuted evolution in his classes. How much worse could this get?

Well, as hard as it is to believe, it does get worse. In a spirit of Christian concern and fairness, brother Swift took from the document that he and his wife were preparing, the section (pp 4.1-4.9) that pertained to their telephone conversation with Archie Manis, and personally (along with one of the Baker Heights deacons) carried it to him for his examination. Then, they provided Dr. Manis with a page on which to write any comments, pro or con, regarding the written log of that telephone conversation. Several things are of interest regarding Dr. Manis' comments, as written in the Swift document by his own hand (section 5 of the document). In section 5, the Swifts had typed at the top of the page the following:

"I, _____, acknowledge by my signature hereon that I have been given the opportunity to read the statements (4.1-4.9) concerning my discussion with L.D. and Dana Swift. Furthermore, I

_____ do

_____ do not

consider them accurate as they are written."

In the first blank, Dr. Manis wrote his name. But oddly enough, when it came to indicating whether or not the statements were, or were not, correct, Dr. Manis refused to put a check mark by **either** of the choices. Now either the statements, as recorded in the document by brother and sister Swift **are** correct, or they are **not** correct. Why is it Dr. Manis should be totally unable to indicate one or the other? Could it be because he **knows** that the statements **are** correct, but does not want to have to admit it?!

On that same page (section 5) there is a two-paragraph statement in Archie Manis' own handwriting. In that statement, Manis states that he did not mean to leave the impression that he was a theistic evolutionist. He says that he is a theist; that he believes in God. He says, however, "I do believe in change, and nonrandom gene shifts in populations—that brand or type or definition of evolution—so one might put the words together. But I have never believed that the universe, life, man, and what we call nature ever made itself by an evolutionary process. The Bible says that God made it all, and I've always believed that" (emphasis added).

One might begin to think, from a cursory reading of that statement, that Dr. Manis had completely exonerated himself. But read it again, and this time a bit more closely. Notice that Dr. Manis says he has never believed that the universe, life, man, and nature "made itself by an evolutionary process." So what?! He has completely side-stepped the major issue of this controversy! Brother Swift has already stated, and we have already quoted, that Dr. Manis "believed that God somehow had a hand in the beginning of life on earth" (p 3.3). And so for Dr. Manis to state that he has never believed life "made itself" is to state the obvious. Next, notice that Dr. Manis says, "The Bible says God made it all, and I've always believed that." Yet Manis has already admitted that he doesn't believe what God said, because he specifically stated that he did **not believe** that the days of creation were days as we know them, in spite of weighty testimony from Scripture which states that they were (Exodus 20:11; Genesis 1:5; Genesis 1:14, etc.). So what **does** Dr. Manis mean by his statement that "The Bible says God made it all, and I've always believed that"? Fortunately, one is not left to wonder, because in his own handwriting, Manis informs us. Read carefully the following admissions from the Manis statement.

"It (evolution—BT) is never presented as dogma, but active theory in an unsettled condition. Our teaching at ACU has more[1] presented evolution as an explanation for the world—it has been and is being presented as **a body of scientific thought supported by a body of scientific evidence.** As theory goes, **there is no decisive evidence against any of these viewpoints, from science**" (5.1, emphasis added).

[1]See Appendix

Notice Dr. Manis states that as evolutionary theory goes, "**there is no decisive evidence against**" it. He says that it is presented by him in his classes at ACU as "**a body of scientific thought supported by a body of scientific evidence.**" Question: if there is "**no decisive evidence against it**" and it is "**supported by a body of scientific evidence**"—WHAT DO **YOU** THINK DR. MANIS IS TRYING TO SAY??

One last item in this regard bears mentioning. Dr. Manis has attempted to speak in "scientific lingo" in his response to the Swifts' charges. No doubt he hoped that this would be confusing enough to prevent anyone from clearly understanding what he was trying to say. But it will not work. Notice, for example, Dr. Manis' statement that he believes in "nonrandom gene shifts." Now, compare the following statement which is taken directly from Dr. Manis' own "Evolution Notes" (p 2, #5): "Thus **evolution is the inevitable process** whereby changes in the gene pool, **nonrandom shifts in gene frequency**, are affected" (emphasis added). What did you say, Dr. Manis? "I believe in nonrandom gene shifts." And? "Evolution is the inevitable process whereby nonrandom shifts in gene frequency" occur. Put into an easy-to-understand syllogism, the statements look like this:

1. "I believe in nonrandom gene shifts" (Manis' own handwriting in section 5.1 of the Swift document).

2. "Evolution is the inevitable process whereby changes in the gene pool, **nonrandom shifts in gene frequency**, are affected (Manis' "Evolution Notes," p 2, #5, emphasis added).

3. Conclusion: I believe in evolution.

Again, I would remind you of Manis' statement (quoted above): "**I do believe** in change, and **nonrandom gene shifts** in populations—**that brand or type or definition of evolution.**" If one wishes to see "that type" of evolution explained, I heartily recommend that he consult the widely used book, *Life: An Introduction to Biology* by G.G. Simpson [known as "Mr. Evolution"], C.S. Pittendrigh, and L.H. Tiffany (Harcourt,

Brace, New York, 1957). Chapter 16, "The Elementary Processes of Evolution," contains a detailed explanation of "nonrandom" genetic shifts which are alleged to be necessary for the evolutionary development of organisms. This is the same textbook, I might add, which affirms that evolution is the theory which "rejects the notion that all organisms were designed and created at the beginning of time" (p 26). To the informed person, there simply is no question as to where this ACU teacher stands with reference to evolution. He is a thorough-going **theistic evolutionist**! It is little wonder, then, that Dr. Manis would remark, by his own handwriting in the Swift document, that since he "is a theist," and since he believes in "nonrandom gene shifts," someone "might put the words together." What words, Dr. Manis? The words **theistic evolutionist**! You are right, Dr. Manis. "Someone" has "put the words together"—and from your very own self-incriminating confession. How could it be any other way? Even when you attempt to disguise it in scientific language, it is still decipherable!

The last section (section 7) of the document prepared by Mr. and Mrs. Swift is the conclusions which they have drawn from their conversations with Dr. Manis. In that section, you will find the following statements:

> "**Concerning the teaching of evolutionary theory at ACU without Scriptural refutation**: Dr. Manis stated emphatically and repeatedly in our telephone conversation of October 28, 1985 that he did not ever present material or arguments in class to refute the theory of evolution. He also stated that he presented the material in the class textbook just as it was written and never made comments to indicate his personal convictions concerning the subjects of creation and evolution. We asked Archie why he did not refute the theory in class and he stated that he assumed that his students knew the Bible and had already studied such things before they came to college. He also said that the students were taught the arguments against evolution in the Bible Department at ACU. He indicated that he believed that Bible should be

taught in the Bible Department and that science should be taught in the Science Department. [Again, if such is the case, why does he devote so much time to "creationism" via handouts from atheistic evolutionists attempting to **refute** it?? BT]

"In conclusion we should first point out that the ACU Bible Department does not and cannot present arguments powerful and pertinent enough to refute evolutionary theory as taught in the Science Department. Only men of faith especially trained in that field of science would have the knowledge and skills to accomplish that. So the Bible Department does not and cannot refute the material that Archie presents in his classes.

"Furthermore, Archie does not refute it by his own admission. And finally, the students certainly do not learn it before they come to college! It is therefore obvious that the theories of evolution as taught and distributed by ungodly, unfaithful men of science are being taught at ACU just as they are presented in written form by these men without refutation of any kind from the science classroom. It is beyond my comprehension how Archie could think that a presentation of these powerful and skillful theories of evolutionary scientists without classroom refutation would do no harm to the thinking and faith of students under his charge. I must conclude that this is either a deliberate oversight because he personally believes these theories, or it is surely the grossest sampling of naivete that I have ever witnessed of a man of Archie's education and position in the Church. There must be untold hundreds of young people whose faith in the biblical creation account is shaken and even destroyed by this approach to teaching. Archie Manis has made a very serious error by failing to protect the faith of many young people who were entrusted to his care and training. He must repent of this wickedness immediately and begin from this day forward to rectify this error to the best of his ability. It must be publicly known what he believes and teaches on this matter (pp 7.1, 7.2).

"**Concerning our reaction to the telephone conversation on October 28, 1985 with Archie Manis**: When we called Archie that evening we were both deeply troubled by the events of the distant and recent past with regard to Archie's beliefs. It was our sincere desire to see Archie exonerated if at all possible. Perhaps, we thought, he had changed over the past four years in his position on evolution. As we talked with him we received evasive answers and ambiguous wording that left us both wondering. After the conversation ended, throughout that evening and the next day we pondered that conversation in private and together. It is now our sincere conviction that Archie Manis does believe and teach evolution as fact and that he intends to continue in that belief and teaching. However, we also think it is now going to be very difficult to get him to publicly admit that because his position as an elder and as a professor at ACU is in danger. May God help us all to seek only the truth and not be blinded by anything in this matter. It is very serious and will affect the brotherhood and our children for years to come (pp 7.3, 7.4).

"**Concerning Archie's statement that he believes in the creation account just as it is written in Genesis 1**: This point may appear to be super-critical, but it is actually the reason why Archie has been able to go so long in error and not be detected. Most brethren would ask him simply, 'Do you believe in the biblical creation account?' To this he would answer quite emphatically, 'Yes!' But what does that mean? It really provides very little information about what he really believes. A much better way to ask the question would be, 'Archie, explain your understanding of the creation account in detail.' Now you're likely to learn more. Let's illustrate in another way. Let me ask the reader a simple question. Do you believe in 'justification by faith'? Of course you do! I do too. Now if I asked a Baptist or a Methodist or a Lutheran that same question I'd get the same answer, but it would not have the same meaning. They would mean, 'Yes, I believe in justification by faith' according to Baptist doctrine or the Methodist doctrine, etc. There is no doubt that Archie believes in the creation account of Genesis 1. He said he did, but I'm convinced he doesn't hold the same belief on that subject as I and others do (pp 7.4, 7.5).

"Concerning my own judgment of Archie Manis on my past experience with this man: The complete consequences of our actions in life are never witnessed in full even by ourselves. Those of us who have lived for any time in this world have learned that our actions can sometimes bring great calamity to others and to ourselves. Hence, we learn to move with caution and to be deliberate, even to the point of excess. So it has been with me concerning the issues surrounding Archie Manis. Only very recently have I become wholly convinced of this man's true nature. I have witnessed his evasiveness and ambiguity when questioned about his beliefs with regard to God's Word and evolution. I have witnessed his anger for no apparent reason other than he had been asked to confirm his faith. I have witnessed a sinister determination to teach his students the theories of organic evolution without refutation and without regard for their spiritual welfare. Archie Manis is in my judgment one of the most dangerous miscreants dwelling among God's people I have ever known. He has the astounding ability to disguise his true nature and his true beliefs and to move undetected among the people of God (p 7.5).

"Concerning the harm that Archie is causing to the

faith of young men and women: The statement above would appear very caustic to many people who might read it. But it is not made without reason or meaning. I firmly believe that Archie is bringing great harm to many, many young people. He is deliberately and systematically undermining the faith of his students in order to replace it with faith in evolution. He is doing this with a conviction that he is right. He is very wrong and for that reason must repent. Whether one aids the cause of evil intentionally or from ignorance makes no difference to the outcome. The cause of evil is served in either fashion" (pp 7.5, 7.6).

The document from which these statements was taken has been used by permission of Mr. and Mrs. Swift. Equally important is the fact that the document is in the hands of ACU administration officials. Who could ask for **more** evidence as to what is now going on, and what has been going on for more years than most of us would care to think, in regard to such false teachings? But have ACU officials acted on the document? Have they relieved the professors involved of their teaching duties? Have they kept their word (remember Dean Reeves' statement to Furman Kearley that if documented evidence could be presented showing evolution had been taught without refutation, that the men involved would be fired???)? Again, the answer is a resounding "NO!" Sad, but true.

<hr>

5

The Raging Storm

"Convinced that no *theory of evolution can survive a 6 literal day creation period, I asked the following question: 'Do you believe that God created the heavens, earth, and everything in them in 6 literal days of approximately 24 hours each?' Initially Archie tried to avoid giving a direct answer, therefore I continued to ask the same question until he gave the following answer: 'I think he could have, if he had wanted to, but I don't think that's the way he did it.' ...He stated he* does *teach evolution and does* not *refute it."*

—John Propst
(Former deacon, Baker Heights
Church of Christ, Abilene, Texas
document of December 4, 1985)

"The doctrine of Evolution, if consistently accepted, makes it impossible to believe the Bible."
—Thomas H. Huxley ("Darwin's Bulldog")

It would no doubt be the understatement of the year for us to say that, as a result of this current controversy, things have not been exactly "quiet and peaceful" in Abilene over the past several months. The flurry of events, especially during the months of October and November, 1985 has in many ways "taken the town by storm." I can certainly understand why. Calls have come in to ACU from as far away as Spain, if you can believe it, concerning this controversy. Parents have been, and still are, writing letters and making telephone calls to University administrators. I suppose Dr. C.G. Gray, Vice-President for Academic Affairs (and a man involved in this cover-up from the very beginning) probably stated the matter well when he told the elders of the Grape Street congregation during a November 13th meeting with them, "Our phones are ringing off the wall, our mail boxes are full-to-overflowing, and I'm spending every waking minute on this thing." The Grape Street elders—and I say this to their credit—have attempted to do everything within their power to help bring about a solution to this terrible problem, once they were made aware of it by brother Willeford's participation in the September 13 meeting. More than once they have met, collectively and individually, with University officials, but each time to no avail. In the November 13 meeting with those elders, Dr. Gray told them that the University had done everything possible to prevent the news of this from spreading, but apparently without success. Personally, I think there is more to that statement than even Dr. Gray knew! Concerned brethren **are** writing; they **are** calling; and they **are** unwilling to accept a white-wash of this entire sordid affair.

While the University was practically smothering under the controversy associated with these problems, certain local congregations were also feeling the shock waves. There is, in fact, quite a story to be told regarding the Baker Heights congregation in Abilene where Archie Manis serves as an elder. The facts of the story are these.

During my September 13-15 seminar at the Grape Street congregation in Abilene, unbeknown to me, some of the members of the Baker Heights congregation attended the lectures. Still others secured taped copies of the lessons, since they were unable to attend personally. At the conclusion of the lectures on Sunday, September 15, a man by the name of John Propst introduced himself to me. We spoke briefly, and discovered that we had a mutual friend who was a preacher in the Fort Worth area. During our conversation, I asked John where he worshipped in Abilene. When he replied, "At the

Baker Heights congregation," I asked him this question: "Am I reading Archie Manis wrong?" John said, "Bert, I honestly do not know. He has never mentioned evolution to me. In fact, the subject has never even come up. However, I will be having a meeting with him shortly to find out what he does believe, and I will let you know if you are reading him wrong or not."

On Wednesday, September 25, John Propst did, in fact, meet with Archie Manis in order to discuss these very things with him. That meeting took place at the Baker Heights church building, and lasted approximately two and one-half hours. The reader will no doubt find the content of this particular meeting to be quite interesting. The statements which follow, both about this meeting and others that were to later occur, are taken directly from a document prepared by John Propst from his own notes taken in those meetings, and from eye-witness testimony of those in the meetings. Brother Propst's document (5 pages, single-spaced) is dated December 4, 1985. We quote from it by permission.

> "At my request, Archie met with me in the Baker Heights building following the mid-week services. The meeting lasted approximately two and one-half hours. I had purposed in my heart not to be side-tracked by being drawn into a 'debate' concerning 'evidences' for or against evolution. My sole purpose was to secure from Archie his own true beliefs concerning evolution. Having known Archie for eight years, I chose to let him do the majority of the talking. I merely expressed my concern about the current charges against him, gave him the floor, and sat back and listened.
>
> "Many times, especially with a Christian, we look for and hear only those things that will set our suspicions aside. After 2 hours of listening to Archie enlighten me, I realized that I had heard the 'correct' answers, no matter what my own convictions might have been. (I had not at that time expressed my own beliefs.) He had used phrases and 'buzzwords' that would have satisfied me re-

gardless of my convictions. Every possible answer had been given—each contradictory of the others. I felt it necessary to further solicit a 'direct, simple' statement from Archie of his personal belief concerning creation/evolution.

"Convinced that **no** theory of evolution can survive a 6 literal day creation period, I asked the following question: 'Do you believe that God created the heavens, earth, and everything in them in 6 literal days of approximately 24 hours each?'

"Initially, Archie tried to avoid giving a direct answer, therefore, I continued to ask the same question until he gave the following answer: 'I think he could have, if he had wanted to, but I don't think that's the way he did it.'

"He proceeded to offer many questions and statements to support his beliefs. He made many other statements:
  —He would love to debate Bert Thompson,
  —He would like to get Bert Thompson in a class so he could teach him and 'straighten him out,'
  —He did not answer Bert Thompson's questions because the ACU administrators advised against it, and the questions were 'obviously' designed to 'entrap' him,
  —He stated that he **does** teach evolution and does **not** refute it. He stated that 'evolution is science; creation is religion—I teach science.'

"It was now obvious to me that Archie did, indeed, believe in a theory of evolution. . . .A few days later, I telephoned to inform you that you were indeed reading Archie correctly."

I spoke, by phone, with brother Propst on October 16 regarding the above-mentioned meeting. John indicated that many important things came out of that discussion. But, the importance of the meeting would not become clear until approximately one month later (October 26). Two other men, both deacons at the Baker Heights congregation, had heard of Dr. Manis' teachings as well, and wanted to meet with him. They asked John Propst to attend the meeting, which he agreed to do. The meeting lasted about three hours. At the beginning of the meeting, John asked Dr. Manis (for clarification, so that there would be no 'misquoting' done on John's part) to please rehearse, for these two deacons, what he (Dr. Manis) had told John concerning the creation days **not** being 24-hour periods of time. Dr. Manis told the gentlemen, at the first of the meeting, that John **had** quoted him correctly in stating that he (Manis) believed that God **could** have done it that way, but that he did **not** believe that God **did** create the world and everything in it in six literal 24-hour days. Toward the end of the meeting, however, Dr. Manis began to be visibly distraught by how the meeting was progressing. He grew frantic and in a sudden outburst, said (this quotation is from the Propst December 4 document, already mentioned above): "I didn't want to say this, in fact, I have tried as hard as I can to keep from saying it, but I believe God created everything in 6 literal days. I've believed it since I was 11 years old." To quote John Propst: "I was absolutely shocked! I expressed my disbelief that he would have deliberately misled and deceived me in the first meeting. His only response was, 'I'm sorry.' "

Little wonder John Propst was "absolutely shocked." In the September 25 meeting, John had asked Dr. Manis **specifically** if he believed in a six literal day creation. Manis had stated **specifically** that he did not. At the beginning of this October 26 meeting, John had asked Manis if that was, in fact, correct. Manis had affirmed that it was. Now—just two hours later in the **very same meeting**—Manis completely reverses his story! **Which** story was the **correct** story? Which time did Dr. Manis tell the truth, and which time did he not? To quote from the Propst document:

"Concerning Archie's two contradictory answers: Did he believe God created everything in 6 literal days, or not?

"Question: Why were contradictory answers given?
   —Misunderstanding? (This was eliminated by
    his confirmation earlier.)
   —Change of Mind? (He **said** he had believed it
    since he was 11 years old.)
   —Dishonesty? (This seems to be the **only** op-
    tion remaining.)"

Which time did Dr. Manis tell the truth? John was only to have
to wait another week, and he would have the answer to that
question. On Friday, November 1, John Propst telephoned
Archie Manis to tell him that after much prayerful deliberation,
the only possibility as to an explanation of Manis' conduct
was that he was dishonest. One week later, on Friday, November 8, Archie Manis called John Propst and asked to meet with
him at the Baker Heights church building. This particular meeting lasted two and one-half hours. Here is John Propst's accounting of that meeting.

"At Archie's request, I met with him again at the
building. This meeting lasted two and one-half hours.
This meeting was extremely perplexing. He rambled
a great deal. There seemed to be 2 thoughts that he
wished to present:
   1.   **Sometimes**, some things **might appear** to
        be contradictory.
   2.   For the first time in his life, he had felt
        backed into a corner during the meeting
        of October 26, 1985.
"I deduced that Archie was offering me a choice of
the two as an explanation for his contradictory answers. The first thought seems to be somewhat lacking in substance, so I've discarded it. The second
one is interesting indeed. Perhaps, Archie is telling
us that if he is pressured, he will say whatever you
want him to.

"I sensed that Archie wished to 'set the record
straight,' so I asked him how he would classify himself: creationist, theistic evolutionist, day/age theory,

gap theory, etc. He became very defensive. He stated that the days mentioned in Genesis 1 were God's days and, therefore, of unknown duration. At least, now I knew what Archie really believed. He definitely did not believe that 'evening and morning' were one day!

"I then asked Archie to resign as an elder of Baker Heights rather than bring reproach upon the church. He stated that he had already offered his resignation, but it had been refused. This was very difficult for me to do, as I love Archie very much, and I'm sure it was very painful for him."

Over the next few weeks, John began to dig deeper and deeper into the problems surrounding Archie Manis. In so doing, John came across the Swift document. He, and one other deacon at the Baker Heights congregation who had also attended my lectures, decided that the time had come to act. [NOTE: This second deacon and his wife—who have requested for personal reasons that their names not be used here—met with Archie Manis on Sunday night, November 3 and questioned him extensively regarding his beliefs in evolution. He stated emphatically during this meeting that God had created everything in six literal 24-hour days.] These two deacons could no longer ignore the mounting evidence. They felt they had been deceived by Manis' conflicting statements, and they were not satisfied. Shortly thereafter, these two deacons and their wives asked to meet with the Baker Heights elders. That meeting did take place on November 20, from 8:30 P.M. until midnight. Present in that meeting were all five of the other Baker Heights elders, and Archie Manis.

Little did these inquiring brethren realize what was about to happen. One by one the Baker Heights elders told the two deacons and their wives that they stood behind Archie Manis 100%. To the man, they stated that you could not know if the days of creation were actual days, or eons of time, for the Bible did not mention anything about "hours," and that it was not a matter of great importance as to whether they were literal days or not. They further stated that they did not feel they could bind their "opinion" on others. The entire elder-ship was now in the Archie Manis camp. The unusual thing about that is this—earlier John Propst and his wife had spoken in their home with one of the elders, who affirmed at that time his profound belief in the days of creation as literal, 24-hour periods of time. But, between that meeting and the one on November 20, **something** (someone?) changed his mind! [NOTE: During this November 20 meeting, Manis plainly denied that the days of creation were 24-hour periods. Upon hearing this, the other deacon and his wife who were present (and who had met with Manis on November 3) asked him why, then, he specifically told them that the days of creation **were** 24-hour periods. **Manis' response was that he, like Paul, had "become all things to all men!"** Can you believe that an elder in the church would intentionally distort the truth, and then try to explain it by stating that he was like the great apostle Paul in that he had "become all things to all men"?? Would Paul do such a thing?]

When these two deacons asked the elders to investigate the charges that I, and others, had made, they indicated that they already had, and that the charges, as far as they were concerned, were completely false. John Propst asked them if they had spoken to any specifically named students at ACU who had been involved in bringing these accusations against Archie, and they admitted that they had not. John asked them if they had contacted me. They admitted that they had not. It appeared that they had "investigated" the matter by simply taking Archie Manis' word for it. They had even been sent, individually, a copy of the Swift document, but not even that was sufficient to cause them to investigate further. In fact, the elders stated that they had not even contacted brother Swift to discuss the document!

There was, however, one last item on these two deacons' agenda. It had to do with the accusation that Archie Manis was (to use their words) "dishonest" in his statements of belief concerning whether or not the days of creation were, in fact, 24-hour time periods. Brother Propst informed the elders that Archie had told him one thing in one meeting; Manis then reaffirmed that statement before two witnesses in a later meeting, and shortly thereafter in the same meeting said exactly the opposite before those same two witnesses. Then, at a third meeting in private with John Propst, Manis admitted that he had always believed that the days of creation were **not** literal and that under pressure he had simply panicked and said what he felt they wanted to hear. John Propst asked that the two witnesses (both of them were deacons as well!) be allowed to testify. The elders agreed that they would hear this testimony on Sunday evening, November 24. However, on Sunday **morning**, November 24 (**before** the testimony of the witnesses was even heard on Sunday evening) the elders at Baker Heights made public statements from the pulpit, completely exonerating Archie Manis and stating that the elders stood behind him 100%. Further, said the elders, some from "out of town" had "enlisted" the aid of several persons in the local congregation in regard to this matter.

The meeting on Sunday evening, November 24, did occur. The elder who chaired the meeting asked that nothing said during the meeting would be repeated outside the room. As this book goes to press, the elders have just announced their decision regarding the charges of Archie Manis' dishonesty. They stated that as far as they are concerned, Archie Manis is innocent. It appears he **is** simply "all things to all men."

As a result of these happenings, the two deacons and their families placed in the hands of the Baker Heights elders letters stating that the men were resigning as deacons. As of November 27, the two families severed their relationships with the Baker Heights congregation. The church as a whole has no idea, as this book goes to press, what all has happened. Another sad chapter in the story of the damage done by one man who will not repent of the error of his ways!

At least one bright spot, however, has come from all of this. During his meeting with John Propst on September 25, Dr. Manis boasted that he genuinely wished he could "get Bert Thompson into a public debate" so that he could "straighten him out." John Propst relayed the Manis debate challenge to me, and I was thrilled to accept. In fact, on November 5 (just a few days after I learned of the challenge) I penned a letter to Dr. Manis, which is reproduced below, accepting **his** challenge, and suggesting two possible debate propositions. The same letter was sent to Dr. Kenneth Williams as well, in hopes that he, too, would be willing to meet in honorable public debate over the issues which divide us.

"Dear Dr. Manis:

"Word has just reached me, through some of those involved, that in a recent meeting with one or more of the deacons of the congregation where you are an elder, you stated that you genuinely wished that you could 'get Bert Thompson into a public debate' so that you could 'straighten him out' on several important points related to the current controversy in which you are involved—i.e., the teaching of evolution or theistic evolution to students at Abilene Christian University.

"This brief letter is to inform you, first, that I am extremely happy to learn of your willingness to debate me in an honorable, public forum before inquiring brethren, and second, that I am absolutely thrilled to accept your invitation. My only regret is that you did not have enough courage of your convictions to challenge me personally, rather than boasting, in my absence, of how you would 'straighten me out' in a public debate.

"I hereby accept your challenge to debate, publicly, the matters around which the current controversy is centered, i.e., whether or not theistic and/or organic evolution may be accepted, and promulgated, by a faithful child of God. Enclosed are two different debate propositions for your consideration. Surely one of them will explicate the position which you now hold, considering your current stand on the teaching of evolutionary concepts to impressionable young minds under your tutelage at Abilene Christian University. You will notice that my signature, and today's date are already affixed to the propositions. All that is lacking is your signature. The date(s), place, and other arrangements necessary for the occurrence of such a public debate may be worked out to our mutual agreement at a later time. I will, in light of your recent boast, look forward to receiving the debate proposition(s), signed by you, by return mail in the near future, unless, of course, you do not have the courage of your convictions and prefer instead to make idle threats behind closed doors.
Sincerely,
(signed) Bert Thompson, Ph.D.''

"PS: In the off-chance that neither of the enclosed propositions is acceptable to you, please feel free to form your
own and send it to me for my consideration. I feel certain that we can work out a debate proposition which is
mutually agreeable.

PPS: Copies of this letter are being sent both to Dr. Kenneth
Williams (in hopes that he, too, might be willing to publicly debate the issues that divide us) and to ACU administrators who, no doubt, will be pleased to see that you
are finally willing to debate that which you once denied
that you accepted."

The parties whose signatures appear below agree to
meet in honorable public debate on the following
propositions, as stated. Time, place, and other appropriate details are to be agreed upon so as to be
mutually acceptable to both parties involved.

RESOLVED: The General Theory of Evolution is
compatible with the teaching of the
Bible.

_____

(signed)

_____

(date signed)

RESOLVED: The General Theory of Evolution is
incompatible with the teaching of the
Bible.

Bert Thompson

(signed)

November 5, 1985

(date signed)

The parties whose signatures appear below agree to

meet in honorable public debate on the following propositions. Time, place, and other appropriate details are to be agreed upon so as to be mutually acceptable to both parties involved.

RESOLVED: Theistic evolution [i.e., the common descent of all living forms, except man, from an original source (or sources)] is compatible with the teaching of the Bible.

_____

(signed)

_____

(date signed)

RESOLVED: Theistic evolution [i.e., the common descent of all living forms, except man, from an original source (or sources)] is incompatible with the teaching of the Bible.

_____Bert Thompson_____

(signed)

_____November 5, 1985_____

(date signed)

_____

Shortly after my letter was mailed to Drs. Manis and Williams, the editor of one of the most highly respected journals in our brotherhood, Jerry Moffit of the Shenandoah Church of Christ in San Antonio, and editor of THRUST, heard of Dr. Manis' challenge and wrote him a letter, asking him to consider debating me in the pages of that very journal—for two consecutive issues! The same letter was sent to Dr. Williams. Brother Moffitt's letter is reproduced in its entirety below.

"November 20, 1985

"Dear Brethren,

"Aware of some of the teaching at Abilene Christian University regarding Evolution and Theistic Evolution, I invited Dr. Bert Thompson to expound and defend his views in a debate published in THRUST Magazine. I asked him to supply me with the names of honorable and sincere men who could, as worthy opponents, defend an opposite viewpoint. He supplied me with both your names.

"We have been made aware that Dr. Manis has already agreed to such a debate, and we wanted to formally invite you both to represent your viewpoint in THRUST. THRUST has lent itself to such discussions, and we never add material to support either viewpoint. We make a fair introduction in an editorial, and then we let the debate speak for itself. In THRUST, differing views have been represented by Dr. James Bales and Robert Shank. They found no cause for criticism regarding even-handed treatment in THRUST. Debates of this type, in THRUST, have generally been about 50 pages. However, we are willing to make an exception in this case. We will devote two of our quarterly issues to this subject matter. Thus, two propositions can be discussed, and if you choose, each of you may handle one proposition. The following propositions are acceptable to us, but please feel free to refine them further by corresponding with Dr. Bert Thompson."

RESOLVED: The General Theory of Evolution is incompatible with the teaching of the Bible.

AFFIRM:_____
     Dr. Bert Thompson

DENY:_____
     Dr. Archie Manis or
     Dr. Kenneth Williams

RESOLVED: Theistic Evolution (i.e., the common descent of all living forms, except man, from an original source, or sources) is compatible with the teaching of the Bible.

AFFIRM:_____

Dr. Archie Manis or
Dr. Kenneth Williams

DENY:_____

Dr. Bert Thompson

"We pray that you will consider this formal debate challenge and our invitation to open the pages of THRUST to you as being offered in the spirit of love and the desire that truth be clearly determined. We are sending a copy of this letter to about 50 interested and concerned brethren. If we can help or serve you in any way, please advise us. When propositions are agreed on, I will mail to all parties manuscript requirements which are necessary in THRUST.

In Christian love,
(signed) Jerry Moffitt
Editor of THRUST"

Others in the brotherhood, who are renowned and respected for their stand for Truth, wrote Drs. Manis and Williams, either offering the pages of the journals which they edit for such a debate, or urging the two professors to conduct such a public debate—quickly. Letters began arriving on the ACU campus from such men as Bill Cline, editor of the *Firm Foundation*, Dub McClish, director of the annual Denton, Texas lectureship program and president of Valid Publications, Tommy Hicks, evangelist of the Handley Church of Christ in Fort Worth, Texas, W.N. (Bill) Jackson, evangelist of the Southwest Church of Christ (and director of that congregation's annual lectureship program) in Austin, Texas. In short, letters from all over the country began to pour in to the two professors and ACU administrators. Alas, all efforts to secure an honorable, public debate were doomed to fail. On November 22, Dr. Manis wrote me a two-paragraph letter (the first communication I had received directly from him throughout this entire ordeal!). His note stated:

"Dear Dr. Thompson:

"Your offer to debate is appreciated, but I see neither reason nor need for a debate about either proposition. We have nothing to debate about. You may also be assured that I would have contacted you directly had there ever been an interest on my part in such an enterprise. Thanks for your concern about the welfare of Christian education.

(signed)
Archie L. Manis, Ph.D."

When Dr. Manis' letter arrived, I could not help but be reminded of the letter I had received only a day before from brother Guy N. Woods, former esteemed editor of the *Gospel Advocate* and currently its Query Editor. On November 19, brother Woods wrote me, because he had heard of Dr. Manis' challenge, and of my acceptance. Brother Woods comments were these:

"Dear brother Bert:

"I find recent developments regarding the situation at ACU quite interesting, and I shall be glad to see any further developments. It would indeed be great if a debate would result, but I shall not hold my breath until it does. I predict that the tent will be silently folded and an Arab departure occur! For fifty years this has been my experience with those who boast TO OTHERS of their readiness to debate. . . .

Faithfully,
(signed) Guy N. Woods"

Oh, brother Woods! How wise those many years of fighting error have made you! You could not have been more correct in your assessment of this current situation.

There is so much more that could be told. As the Queen

of Sheba said of the wisdom of Solomon, "I believed not the words until I came, and mine eyes had seen it: and behold, the half was not told me. . ." (I Kings 10:7). Surely, the "half hath not been told." The story could indeed be lengthened, simply by telling of all of the people who remain unnamed, even though they have quietly, behind-the-scenes, stood firmly for the Truth of God. Or, mention could be made of students, and parents, and grandparents, and aunts and uncles, who have prayed fervently daily that our efforts to correct these many errors might be successful. But these things would only detract from the importance of the message that has been told. And that message is this: Evolution—undiluted infidelity—has been, and is being, taught to students under these two professors, and that without refutation. The trust which parents have so lovingly given to the Abilene Christian University has been prostituted. Parents and students alike have been betrayed, and in a most insidious way. Souls of young people—sent to ACU for the purpose of being built up and strengthened—have been endangered through the teaching of this dogma of evolution as if it were just another scientific "fact" like apples falling off trees. But—and this is perhaps most important of all—the entire tragic series of events would have been simply papered over and covered up had it not been for the dauntless faith of a few who would not—despite the pleas of some—come down "to the plain of Ono" (Nehemiah 6:2) to compromise the inspired, inerrant, authoritative word of God.

It is our sincere hope that the sacrifices of the people mentioned in this book—who stood for right and against wrong—will not be in vain. It is our fervent prayer that the great brotherhood of which we are proudly a part will no longer play the role of the sleeping giant, but instead will awake and demand accountability from the Goliath who thinks that accountability is no longer necessary. Some have forgotten: it is not always the "biggest" who win. God does not always count size, or even numbers. His yardstick of success is now, always has been, and forever will be, FAITHFULNESS (Revelation 2:10). Nothing more, nothing less, will suffice.

6

One Last, Futile Effort
To Communicate

"We parents put our children into the hands of 'Christian' professors at a 'Christian' University feeling confident that their faith will be strengthened, not weakened. That is what makes this all so ludicrous. 'They sneaked up on our blind side.' The terrible tragedy is, how many students out there have faith problems now because these two men and their superiors did this to them or allowed it to happen to them. I am just sick about this...."

—Mrs. Jerry (Rowena) Lobley
(Texline, Texas)
(Letter of December 2, 1985)

"We stand either with God and His teaching of creation, or we stand with the evolutionist in opposition to Him. The issues are sharply drawn; there can be no compromise. You are either a Christian or an evolutionist; you cannot be both."

—Dr. G. Richard Culp
(**Remember Thy Creator**, 1975, p 163)

On November 1, 1985 what was intended to be our final communication with ACU regarding this matter was mailed. It was our letter to Dr. Gray (which has been reproduced elsewhere in this book—see page 107) indicating that since ACU apparently had no intention of providing the documents from the two professors, as specified, there obviously remained little else to say. This chapter is included in this book so that people will know that we went "the second mile" with ACU in an attempt—though doomed—to find an equitable solution to this very serious problem of the teaching, **without refutation**, of evolution at ACU.

On November 7, 1985 Mr. Dub Orr, member of the Board of Trustees of ACU (one of the four men present in the original September 13 meeting on the ACU campus) penned a personal letter to me. The gist of the letter, which was, by the way, very kind, was this: please do not shut off communications with ACU. The letter stated that since I had flown to Abilene in September to meet with ACU officials, Mr. Orr would be happy to fly to Montgomery, or Dallas, or wherever else might be necessary so that we could discuss these issues again, in hopes of finding a solution. As it turned out, I was to be in Dallas on November 15-17, presenting a creation/evolution seminar at the Webb Chapel congregation. I telephoned Mr. Orr and told him that I would be most happy to meet with him in Dallas on Sunday afternoon, November 17, after all of my weekend presentations had been completed. I told him, however, that due to the fact that there were apparently some kind of "misunderstandings" on **exactly** what was said in the September 13 meeting (as evidenced by the fact that the two professors' documents contained nothing even remotely resembling what **should** have been in them), I would be bringing my tape recorder, so that the meeting could be recorded. In this way, I explained to brother Orr, there would be no doubt about what was, or what was not, said. I also informed him that I would gladly provide him with exact duplicates of the tapes, for his use(s). Brother Orr thanked me for my willingness to meet, and told me that he would be happy to meet with me under the conditions specified. He asked if Mr. Lynn Packer, Chairman of the ACU Board of Trustees, could attend the meeting with him. I told him that I would **welcome** having Mr. Packer at the meeting. The next day, brother Orr telephoned me again. He informed me that he had spoken to brother Packer, and that brother Packer adamantly refused to meet with me if there was going to be a tape recorder. I was somewhat surprised, and asked brother Orr if brother Packer had something to hide that he didn't particularly want on tape? Brother Orr said simply that Lynn Packer would not come to the meeting if it was to be recorded. I told Dub Orr that, in that case, I would not expect Mr. Packer at the meeting. I did remind Mr. Orr, however, that he had **already agreed** to the conditions, as specified, and he acknowledged that he had. He stated that he would come anyway, and I said that I would see him in Dallas on that Sunday afternoon at the Webb Chapel building at approximately 1:30 P.M. Upon my arrival in Dallas on Friday afternoon, November 15, the church secretary handed me a message from Mr. Orr, stating that Dr. Ian Fair, Dean of the College of Biblical Studies at ACU (and another participant in the September 13 meeting) would be coming with him.

On Sunday afternoon, November 17 I did, in fact, meet with these two brethren at the Webb Chapel church building. Many different items were discussed in that meeting, but at the end of the meeting it was crystal clear to both sides that no solution had been reached. The meeting (which lasted approximately 2½ hours) did, however, produce what I think are some most interesting bits of information which relate to the current controversy. This chapter of the book documents not only our willingness to keep the lines of communication open (as evidenced by my readiness to alter my flight schedule in order to stay in Dallas for the meeting), but also documents those pieces of information which will help the reader to better understand why the situation at ACU is now as it is. We think you will find the following items of paramount importance. [Quotations are verbatim quotes from the taped meeting.]

At the outset of the meeting, I was attempting to explain to brethren Orr and Fair that I did not believe ACU fully understood the magnitude and ramifications of this particular matter, and that the serious nature of the false teachings of the two professors had apparently not "sunk in." Brother Orr responded to my statement as follows [NOTE: The designations for the speakers are: D.O. = Dub Orr, I.F. = Ian Fair, and B.T. = Bert Thompson]:

D.O.: "Our problem is, Bert, that we see the hearsay things and we see the quotes and we have the knowledge of the kind of person we know Archie [Manis—BT] to be over the last 10 years or whatever, and these don't line up. And when he looks us in the eye and says 'I do not believe in evolution,' and he reads publicly the Genesis account and says this is what the eldership at Baker Heights believes, I tend to put more credibility in that, given the fact that his life is lined up with that than I do in things that—well, such as brother Swift has remembered after 3 or 4 years. And uh, therefore, I have a conflicting thing that if we knew he was a hypocrite and a bad guy, then it would be easy to say, 'Archie, we're through with you,' but we know the sort of loving person he is and we don't see that he has subverted a great number of kids with whatever he's done. He's accused of being in the subversion business now for ever since he's been at ACU. Well, in my own knowledge, I don't know of any kid—I'm sure there has been because there's been so many come through—but I know of no student that has lost his faith as a result of Archie's classes. I've known of some that felt that he did not properly present it. Dale Burleson told me that that was the way he felt. Apparently Brenda Lobley feels that way. There are probably others, but I still know of no one that he has been successful in converting to evolution."

B.T.: "And so because he's been unsuccessful, you'll just let him go—right?"

D.O.: "No, we're not going to let him go. We're just going to say that the damage is limited. We're not looking at a major subversion of the entire brotherhood out of what he's done in the classroom. If he was trying to teach evolution as a fact, he's done a very poor job, because he hasn't converted anybody that we know of. Do you know of anybody that has actually lost their faith as a result" [Bert Thompson interrrupts].

B.T.: "No sir. No, I can't name a one yet. Not one yet, but of course my research is continuing and it **will be** heavy-duty, you can bank on it. As you already have said, I've

-148-

done my homework and you'd better believe I'm going to keep it up."

The implications of this conversation surely will not escape the reader. The attitude (and this attitude will be expressed once again later in this very document) is this: Once we have seen that a youngster has **lost** his (or her) **faith** as the result of the teaching of evolution by Dr. Manis, **then** (and only then) will we do something about it. Talk about shutting the barn door **after** the cow has gotten out?! This is the classic example! Is that what it is going to take for people to understand the serious nature of this matter—for young people to actually **lose their souls** before the false teaching is stopped? Is it not enough that Mr. & Mrs. Jerry Lobley of Texline, Texas called and wrote to complain to the University that their daughter had "faith problems" because of the teachings of Dr. Manis (and notice that Mr. Orr even referred to their daughter, Brenda, in his statement!)? Is it not enough that Dale Burleson of Oskaloosa, Iowa had telephoned Mr. Orr to tell him, that Dr. Kenneth Williams taught him, **in 1972**, evolution as if it were factual, **without refutation**? Is it not enough that Dr. Manis **admits** (in the Swift document) to teaching evolution **without refutation**? What will it take, brethren, for the magnitude and ramifications of this problem to finally "settle in" on ACU? The answer: give us one lost soul and **then** we'll believe you! God forbid!

Shortly after this discussion, the topic turned to whether or not ACU was, in fact, trying to "correct" the situation. The two ACU officials said that "something" was going to be done. I asked if that was indeed the case, why weren't the statements from the two professors forthcoming as promised in the September 13 meeting?

B.T.: "I gave you the opportunity to correct it. I gave you six weeks, and you did not correct it."

D.O.: "It's not corrected as you define it, but we're moving toward correcting it. But then it goes back to this credibility problem we have that you don't trust us to correct it."

B.T.: "No sir, I don't because I haven't seen any evidence that you are. I'm saying, in fact, the documents you sent were next to nothing. They weren't even what was asked for in the meeting. I can't believe it."

D.O.: "As I define it, as I was in the meeting, that's what was asked for. You say I'm acting in bad faith because I remember it my way. I could as well say you're acting in bad faith because you remember it your way."

B.T.: "Yes, you could say that. **Fortunately**, for everybody concerned, fortunately there was a neutral witness present, fortunately. And his name is brother James Willeford. And fortunately I happen to have from brother Willeford an eight-page single-spaced document, written shortly after he got out of the meeting, that I would like to read a portion of to you, just so you know the significance, the importance, of this matter, which, I repeat, I don't seem to have gotten over to you. I want to read you a portion of this. I'd like to read it uninterrupted, with your permission."

At that point, I read from the Willeford document. And, I read each of the seven points which were stated in the September 13 meeting as necessary to be in the professors' statements. Those points have already been listed in this book (pp 83,84), and so they will not be repeated here. My point in reading the Willeford document was this: It is **not** a matter of one person's word against another's—as Mr. Orr wanted to make it seem. Instead, there **was** a neutral, independent witness present who **confirmed** exactly what should have been in the documents.

Another interesting point bears on this one. When Mr. Orr called to ask for the meeting, I asked him to bring one specific item with him to the meeting. I asked him to bring the notes which Dr. Fair had taken at the original meeting. Why did I request such? For this reason: during the September 13 meeting, I listed the items that were to be in the documents, and I listed them **twice**. After repeating them, I asked Dr. Fair if he had the items in his notes. He assured me that he did. So, I thought it would be interesting to see what he did, in fact, write down. Mr. Orr looked at Dr. Fair and said:

D.O.: "You might review what your notes say about the meeting, Ian."

I.F.: "But my notes were intended just as sketch notes for my benefit and I just have here, 'Thompson—Define term evolution, I don't believe in organic evolution, progressive creation, theistic evolution, do not advocate,' and then I have four dots."

B.T.: "There's not one word in any of these documents [from the two professors—BT] about theistic evolution which you and I both know, Ian—you and I both know—is my main concern here. When a professor from ACU writes me a note and says 'I don't believe in organic evolution,' great day, fellows, don't you think I know that?! I mean these men are supposed to be—if you're telling me the truth—they're supposed to be Christians. One of them is at least allegedly an elder in the church. Alright, if a guy writes me and says, 'I don't believe in organic evolution,' that doesn't tell me anything. What I want to know is, are you a theistic evolutionist?"

My point to the two men was this: The documents from the two professors were supposed to have contained specific points—which would have settled this matter once and for all. Instead, the professors sent nebulous statements (reproduced elsewhere in this volume) that contained almost none of the specifics. Why? I suggest that it is because the professors **couldn't** sign such statements, knowing they would have been out-and-out lies! Their statements that "I believe in God and Jesus and the Holy Bible" say nothing. Any denominationalist could say the same thing!

As the conversation continued, the one thing that had become apparent to me long, long ago—at the outset of this investigation—suddenly became all the clearer. Mr. Orr spoke up to say:

D.O.: "What you do as far as the school is concerned in your publications at this point is not going to cause us to do anything more or anything less. Once it's come to our attention, we're going to do a better job of teaching."

My comments to these statements, in the context of what was being said, were these:

B.T.: "You see—let me stop you there Dub and interrupt you because I have to put this in—and I know you'll disagree with it and I respect your right to disagree. The attittude you've just expressed is what irks me that most about this thing. 'We are above you. We are above any questioning. You know, no matter what you do, or what anybody else does, we don't have to answer to you. And what you do is not going to affect us one way or the other.' I **disagree** with you strongly. I think the brotherhood is a sleeping giant, and when they see the evidences at hand—not the hearsay, I don't deal in hearsay—when they see the documented evidences I think the people at the University are going to have to take an entirely different attitude and that is, 'We **do** have to answer to you. You're the people who fund us; we have prostituted your trust. You have sent us your children, we have taught them evolution.' I think that you're going to have to see that you can't have that attitude!"

D.O.: "We have **not** taught them evolution."

B.T.: "You **have** taught them evolution. Archie admitted it. It's in the [Swift] document."

D.O.: "We taught them evolution as an academic discipline. We have not taught it as a fact."

B.T.: "Wrong! No sir. You are wrong in that."

D.O.: "But back to my original statement. Whether you believe it or not, I know the ACU Board, and to a degree I know the administration. They are men that are going to correct what we conceive as being wrong, but they are not going to be a group that would accept that there has to be draconian measures taken against people that we've seen to be able to give good service to the Lord."

So there you have it. The University is not prepared to take any kind of "draconian measures" against these men. They are false teachers; they have prostituted the trust given to them by parents by teaching evolution as factual to the students. Yet no "draconian measures" are necessary. Interesting, isn't it? A man can write "myth" across Genesis 1. He can admit to teaching evolution **without refutation**. Charges that he is dishonest can be brought against him by deacons at the congregation where he is an elder. And yet no "draconian measures" are necessary! What next?

But Dr. Fair spoke up to complain that he himself had spoken to Archie Manis, and that Archie had denied any wrong-doing.

I.F.: "We, again, you are saying that we are not willing to react to the evidences. We don't have all the evidence. As much as we've got we've looked at. From what I've got I've sat down and talked to Archie and said, 'Do you believe this?' and Archie says, 'No.' I don't know what else I can do about that."

B.T.: "I've got to comment on that, Ian, I've got to."

I.F.: "Do!"

B.T.: "I'm going to, because this is a **classic**. And again, it's not hearsay. It was with Archie present. In one meeting with one of the deacons [at Baker Heights—BT], John Propst—and I have permission to use John's name— John asked Archie, he said, 'Archie, do you believe that God created the things in six literal 24-hour days as per Genesis 1?' Archie said, 'I believe God **could** have done it that way, but He did not.' He said He used a 'long expanse of time.' He took 'processes' and so on and so on. OK. The meeting lasted for three hours roughly. About two weeks later some more of the deacons at Baker Heights got wind of it. They came to Archie, said 'would you meet with us—we'd like to talk this over.' Archie said, 'You bet.' They asked John Propst to just come and sit in. So John at the beginning of the meeting said, 'Now Archie, I just want to make sure I didn't misquote you. You did say to me—in this meeting when you and I were just in this meeting alone, you did **not** believe the days of creation were 24-hours, you believe God used vast processes and so on.' And Archie said, 'That's right.'

OK. At the end of the meeting Archie got very upset, very violent—as you yourself [Dub Orr] indicated that he could do sometimes, and he said, 'I didn't want to have to tell you this'—and there were three witnesses present, brethren— he said, 'I didn't want to have to tell you this, but I have believed those days of creation were 24-hour days since I was eleven years old.' John said, 'Wait a minute, Archie, you told me in the front of this meeting you didn't believe that, and you told me 2½ weeks ago for three hours you didn't believe that.' He said, 'Which is it that you really believe?' Well, they all left the meeting befuddled. Then, Friday night a week ago, Archie says, 'Would you come meet with me again, John?' John says, 'Sure I will, Archie.' So they went and met over at the church building, across from John's house. Archie said, 'John I just wanted to call you and tell you that you know what I said the other day about me believing in the six literal 24-hour days,' he said, 'that's not true; I don't believe that.' He said, 'I never have believed it. I just wanted to call and tell you I just got under pressure and I said some things I just shouldn't have said, and I just don't believe that.'

"You're telling me that you trust the fellow who in the middle of a heated discussion will just lie to you? Just out-and-out say, 'I believe it. I've believed it since I was eleven years old' and then guilt sort of begins to weigh down on him so the next week he calls up and says, 'I really don't believe that, you know.' And I've got the documentation on it!

"Now fellows, why cannot we clear this up? I mean—do you not—is it because no one has the power? Is it because they are just going like this [waving arms to face] —monkey see, monkey do—see no evil, hear no evil? I mean this stuff gets more rotten every single day."

D.O.: "If you were, if you were going to clear it up, how would you clear it up?"

B.T.: "I would fire those two professors, today. I told you that meeting [September 13—BT] —you've got a **serious** problem here of absolutely mammoth proportions. I tried to get that over to you."

Apparently even this was not enough, however, to get my point over. Mr. Orr's comments shortly thereafter were these:

D.O.: "Do you know of anybody that has taken that teaching [of evolution] and become an evolutionist out of it?"

B.T.: "Dub you can't say that. That's not fair."

D.O.: "If it was a **major** problem, I think we would have heard about it. My only problem is that I'm still trying to keep this in the proper perspective and that is that because we've got a couple of blighted trees, the whole forest is not damaged."

B.T.: "You teach evolution without refuting it, it **is a MAJOR** problem! PERIOD! Whether some kid out there accepts it and takes it home and imbibes it with his mother's milk is beside the point. Besides, who's to know that there aren't some like that?"

D.O.: "It's certainly an error, but it is not a "hanging offense" is what I'm trying to say."

B.T.: "No sir, disagree! It is definitely, to use your words, a 'hanging offense.'"

So you see, once again we come to the lack of understanding about the magnitude of the problem! But nothing explains how University officials feel about the problem any better than the statements which follow. Read them and weep:

D.O.: "I agree with you. Sin is sin. Anything that is a falling-short of God's ideal is unacceptable and is sin. But as to the effect, there are different measures of seriousness. In simple terms you know if I wrongly embezzle some money from my employer—so-called 'white-collar' crime—that's wrong and I've sinned. But the effect is not quite as violent as if I get out and shoot somebody and murder them. That's also a sin. But the effects are much graver in the murder sin than in the white-collar

-155-

sin. And that's the point I'm trying to make in the context of ACU. The effect—sin is sin—but the effects have not been as grave as they could have been—perhaps due to God's grace—and therefore I think perhaps you can handle white-collar sin in a little different way than you would handle a murderer that is out there somewhere. And that's what I was trying to make the point about our handling of this matter at ACU.

At this point in the conversation, brethren Fair and Orr both spoke up to point out that actually the "damage" would be much less if a Christian—in a Christian University setting—were teaching these evolutionary concepts because the students would see him going to chapel everyday, would see him worshipping on Sunday, would see him generally in the "Christian College" context. I, on the other hand, wanted to point out an entirely different viewpoint. My words were these:

B.T.: "I suggest to you—and I hope you'll understand where I'm coming from—and I suggest to you the potential for danger is **even more insidious because they are in a Christian environment**, because the kids are where they should be protected, they're not 'on-guard.' You send them into a professor's office or classroom, he teaches them theistic evolution and/or organic evolution as fact, without refutation, and the net effect is the kid's got his guard down, the kid's there, he's **vulnerable**, his parents are paying for it [Dr. Fair interrupts] ."

I.F.: "But they haven't been too successful in doing that, because we just haven't got a whole bunch of theistic evolutionists running around on campus."

B.T.: "You don't know that!"

I.F.: "Oh, I have them [the kids] in my classes. And believe me, if it was a problem out there, then those questions would be raised in our classes."

B.T.: "I somewhat disagree with you, Ian, and let me tell you why. Because of the very point that Dr. Reeves [Dean of the College of Natural and Applied Sciences—BT] tried to make to me in that meeting September 13 when he said, 'But don't you think it's a little odd that no one's raised the red flag, no one's said anything to us about this before?' And I will tell you now just like I told him then. I don't think it's odd one bit, when Manis comes along and the one kid that does raise his hand and says something, he gets his grade lowered. I don't think it's odd at all!''

D.O.: "His grade was—that was reversed."

B.T.: "I know it, but it was still lowered, and they're not going to get around that."

D.O.: "Institutionally it was handled. On the Manis level it was obviously a thing that had to be corrected."

B.T.: "Why, it certainly did, or the accrediting people would come down on you so hard you wouldn't even believe it. And Mark Scott knows that!"

D.O.: "But it wasn't fear out of any accrediting people, it was just the right thing to do."

The point—and I think it was made quite well—was this: If **you** were a student at ACU, would **you** speak up (knowing what has happened to people like Mark Scott who had his grades lowered when he **did** stand up and say something)? You be the judge! Think of the pressure that these kids are under as they strive to successfully complete their education. And so that the reader will understand first-hand the very points that I was trying to make regarding the potential damage which can be done to the students because they are not "on-guard," we offer the following **unsolicited** letter which addresses this very point. The letter was written December 2, **1985** by Mrs. Rowena Lobley of Texline, Texas (you will remember it was her daughter, Brenda, who suffered "faith problems" because of the teachings of Manis and Williams). Mrs. Lobley wrote:

"Thank you so much for the copy of James Willeford's notes. Brenda was here the day they came, and she affirmed again that **never** was evolution refuted by Dr. Manis!. . . .She said her faith had suffered. We parents put our children into the hands of 'Christian' professors at a 'Christian' University feeling confident that their faith will be strengthened, not weakened. That is what makes this all so insidious. 'They sneaked up on our blind side.' The terrible tragedy is, how many students out there have faith problems now because these two men **and** their superiors did this to them or allowed it to happen to them. I am just sick about this. . ." (emphasis in original).

We rest our case!

As the meeting on November 17 was about to adjourn, there was one last point that I wanted to cover. Only a few short days before, Dr. Archie Manis had boasted to one of the deacons at the Baker Heights congregation in Abilene that he would like to "get Bert Thompson into a public debate and straighten him out" on these issues. As you already know from previous pages in this book, upon learning of that debate challenge (though made in the form of a private boast), I gladly accepted, and wrote Archie Manis a letter telling him so. In light of that event, my statements to the two brethren were these.

B.T.: "I have one other question before we go, real quickly. I'd kind of like an explanation for this because I haven't heard one. Of course, I don't think I'm ever going to get it in writing, that's for sure. But Archie—in front of witnesses—and you say he's innocent, or at least he's not teaching evolution as a fact—I'm a little curious then why he would tell the deacons at Baker Heights, 'Boy,' he said, 'I sure would love to get Bert Thompson into a public debate and clean his plow and straighten him out on some of these things.' You know, if he and I are so much in agreement, what is it he's got to 'straighten me out' on?"

I.F.: "I have no idea."

D.O.: "I have read your letter. I don't know the context. If he said that he's guilty of terrible diarrhea of the mouth, just like he's been all along."

I.F.: "I don't question whether he said it; he no doubt said it, but why [Dr. Fair is interrupted by Mr. Orr]."

D.O.: "He's crazy!"

I.F.: "That's uh—unless—and I have to agree from your standpoint, unless he feels that he's right and you're wrong in this theistic evolution. Alright?"

B.T.: "Yes!"

I.F.: "That's the one alternative. The other one is that he might not have in mind this evolution thing at all. I don't know. I don't know."

I find all of this interesting, to say the least. And, were it not a matter of such serious, eternal consequences, I might even laugh at it. First Archie Manis wants to debate me only because he's got "diarrhea of the mouth, just like all along." Or, second, he wants to debate me because "he's crazy." Or, third, he wants to debate me because he "feels he's right and I'm wrong" on theistic evolution. What wonderful traits for an ACU professor to have!

As I have said before, so say I now again: This stuff gets more rotten every single day!

7

Desperate Measures

"To those who are trained in science, creationism seems like a bad dream, a sudden reliving of a nightmare, a renewed march of an army of the night risen to challenge free thought and enlightenment.... Creationism, on the other hand, is not a theory. There is no evidence, in the scientific sense, that supports it. Creationism, or at least the particular variety accepted by many Americans, is an expression of early Middle Eastern legend. It is fairly described as 'only myth.' "

—Dr. Isaac Asimov
Foremost humanist/evolutionist author
In: **Science and Creationism** (edited by evolutionist Dr. Ashley Montagu)—the text required by Archie Manis in his spring, 1985 ACU biology seminar class

"There are hundreds of professors who have wiggled their way into universities by saying that they believe the Bible, but who really meant by that, that they believe some kind of inspiration like Shakespearean inspiration, and they had no problem with the Bible containing myth and legend.... Whenever one uses such terms as 'hymn,' 'theological language,' 'myth,' and so forth, beware—he is simply saying that it doesn't mean what it

says, that it is not literally true."

—Dr. Furman Kearley
Editor, **Gospel Advocate**, Formerly
Director of Graduate Bible Studies
Abilene Christian University; in a
letter to Mr. Dub Orr, ACU Board
member, (November 11, 1985, p 3)

"When I use a word, it means just what I choose it to mean, neither more nor less."

From **Alice in Wonderland**

This "last chapter" is by necessity, not design. It may be considered somewhat of an epilogue, or a "P.S." of sorts. Actually, it was never intended to be written. But it has been, and oddly enough, not so much by this writer, as by those at Abilene Christian University. Perhaps a word of explanation is in order.

As this book was originally designed, the preceding chapter was intended to draw a close to our comments on this sad series of circumstances, thus, its title, "One Last, But Futile, Effort To Communicate." The text of this book was written during the latter parts of November and the early parts of December, 1985. **Not a single word was put into print for this book before November 15, 1985!** Why? Simple: October 31, 1985 was the deadline, as agreed to by all parties in the September 13, 1985 meeting at ACU, for the two professors' statements regarding these matters to arrive in my office. I honestly believed the University officials when they said they would provide the documents as specified in that meeting. I was wrong, of course, in that belief. But at the time I simply took the men at their word. For that reason, I wrote not a word of this book. I had sincerely hoped that it would not even be necessary. Again, I was badly mistaken.

Toward the middle of November, as it became apparent that ACU officials had no intention of providing the documents from the two professors, as specified in the September 13 meeting, work began on this book. During the weeks in which this volume was in preparation, a flurry of events occurred— many of which are ultimately of extreme importance regarding the outcome of this controversy. As details of those events became available, we filed them away, knowing they needed to somehow be reported. Rather than return and re-write certain portions of the book, we have elected to simply pen a final chapter dealing with these various events which are sometimes connected, sometimes unconnected, to each other. Because of the **nature** of the events, we have chosen to call this chapter, "Desperate Measures." As you will shortly note, the events herein reported do indeed represent "desperate measures" on the part of ACU professors and administrators, as they scurried here and there attempting to exonerate themselves and at the same time cover up the serious errors that had occurred, both in teaching and in tactics.

For convenience and ease of understanding, we have elected to identify and discuss these "desperate measures" by means of major subheadings. There is no particular chronological order, and no order of importance. Each event discussed is crucial to an understanding of the magnitude of the current problem at ACU, and will help the reader to see how the problem has been "handled" all along. Consider, if you will, the following items.

The Student Petition

One of ACU's "defenses" in their indefensible mishandling of this case is the Student Petition which attempts to exonerate professors Williams and Manis of the charges against them. The text of the Petition is reproduced below. Please read it carefully in preparation for the analysis which follows.

"To all biology students:

"As you may know, a student on this campus and some adults (who are not connected with the school) are trying to have Dr. Archie Manis and Dr. Ken Williams removed from their positions as professors at ACU. It is alleged that these men have taught evolution as a fact, and have forced students to believe it. Churches across the state have been alerted that these ACU professors are using 'Satan's tool' (evolution) and tainting the faith of ACU students. The students are the only defense these two men have. The administration is supporting our teachers, but none of them were actually in the classroom, so they cannot say without a doubt that these men are innocent. It is up to people who have had either or both of these professors to renounce the accusations against them.

"There is something else you can do to help besides signing this petition. Please write a letter to the Vice-President of Academic Affairs, Dr. C.G. Gray, (ACU Box 7818, or drop it off at his office, across from Dean Archibald's office, or give it to me.) stating anything you can think of that might be helpful. For instance, in both classes I had under these teachers, each man stated that he believed God made the world. If you remember the same type thing, please say so in your letter. This is **urgent**. Personal statements from the ACU biology students will be very helpful (and it's also our only hope). Please see the attached sheet, and sign it if you are in agreement with its terms.

Thank you very much,
Name Withheld

P.S. There is an example of a good letter stapled to the back of this."

There are several things about the foregoing document that should be noted. Let us begin by pointing out that this Petition was authored by a young woman, a biology major who became emotionally caught up in this controversy as its pressures began to produce telling effects upon one of the professors involved. [Note: we are withholding the young lady's name because we believe that she is a victim—a victim of her own lack of biblical expertise, a victim of the professors' influence, and a victim of the administration's manipulation. We do not wish to see her embarrassed or hurt.] In an interview subsequent to the circulation of this Petition, this student declared[1] that as this controversy began to intensify, she noted a remarkable change in professor Manis' disposition. She said it was apparent that this thing was making him physically ill and, to use her words, "It broke my heart." She confessed that she wanted to do something to help, hence she got the idea to circulate the Petition, the design of which was to help Williams and Manis in their predicament—particularly to assist in saving their jobs, which she felt were threatened. However, in so doing the naive young woman becomes an unwitting witness **against** these teachers.

There are several items in the Petition that should be carefully noted. First, she states. "It is alleged that these men have taught evolution as a fact. . . ." No, that is not the case. Nothing has been **alleged**. For example, Manis brags that he teaches evolution. His own "Evolution Notes" declare that "the fact of evolution is beyond dispute." As Eliphaz said, "Thine own mouth condemneth thee, and not I; Yea, thine own lips testify against thee" (Job 15:6). In view of the fact that her Petition denies that Manis and Williams have "taught evolution as a fact," the young lady was asked in the interview with Dub McClish, how she explained the statement from Manis' "Evolution Notes" that "the fact of evolution is beyond dispute." She responded:

> "Well, you know, goodness, I feel—I mean, I got those notes and scanned them, but I **never read them very closely.**"

The reader hardly needs our help in assessing the credibility of this testimony. Again, note this regarding the Manis' quote:

> "I can't say why he made that quote, and I've worried that he may not be able to say either."

---

[1] Shortly after the distribution of this Petition, Dub McClish, a well-known and highly respected preacher of Denton, Texas, obtained a copy of it. He phoned the young lady who authored the document and conducted an extensive interview with her. That interview was tape recorded (with her knowledge) and the quotations herein referred to are taken from that tape.

And if that were not enough, listen to this statement from this one who is attempting to clear Dr. Manis.

> "He [Manis] has a hard time answering a question 'yes' or 'no'. And I don't know if you've been in any of the discussions with him, but sometimes when Mark [Scott] would ask him point-blank, 'Are you an evolutionist?', well, I mean, he just would start kind of rambling. He's a good man, but he does have some trouble communicating."

We submit that Manis has "communicated" in a perfectly clear fashion! And that communication finally caught up with him!

Second, we have not asserted that students were "forced" to believe in evolution (though one student claimed that the dogma was being "crammed down" their throats). We **have** argued (and with ample proof) that: (a) Rank evolution has been taught in these ACU science classes (with no refutation); (b) The doctrine of creation, with its biblical and scientific support, was never presented to the students; rather, it was ridiculed, and material antagonistic to it was introduced in abundance; (c) Anyone daring to oppose this lopsided procedure was threatened with reprisal. Just these insignificant items!

In connection with point (b) above, in the McClish interview the young woman was asked:

> "Do you ever recall being given any copies, notes, or handouts, or things of that kind, in your botany or biology classes, showing the fallacies and weaknesses of evolutionary models, and the strengths of the creation model?"

Here is the honest response.

> "I can't say that I remember."

Of course, as we have shown elsewhere in this book, Manis himself has admitted that he never gave materials showing the fallacies of evolution.

Third, the Petition denies that the professors' teaching has "tainted the faith" of ACU students. However, when the young lady was confronted with the concrete evidence of a former ACU student who suffered serious "faith problems" because of her exposure to evolution at the University, she exclaimed:

"Oh my goodness—I was not aware of that. I don't know what to say. I should know those things because I've been so active in it."

She went on to observe that she felt the "majority" who passed through the science department were not hurt by the instruction. Our question is this: just **how many** have to be damaged before it becomes a problem?! Moreover, as we shall presently observe, it is rather obvious that not even this young lady's faith is what it could (and should) have been after instruction for more than three years in a Christian university.

Fourth, why is it claimed that "the students are the only defense these two men have"? Do not the teachers have handouts, class notes, textbooks, etc.,—supporting creation and condemning evolution—to introduce in their favor? Not one page has ever come to light! And why are the students divided on this issue? Do some of them know who's "buttering their bread"? What did those students who testified against the professors have to gain by such action?

Fifth, the Petition states: "each man [Manis and Williams] stated that he believed God made the world." If this were not so serious, it would be laughable. Any theistic evolutionist on earth will affirm his belief that "God made the world." That statement says only one thing—the men are not outright atheists—and that's all it says. These people must think that our brethren are extremely dense!

The McClish interview revealed one thing very clearly: this impressionable ACU student has no idea as to what "theistic evolution" actually involves and, in fact, one of her statements indicates that she herself is not without some "taint" in this matter. Note this statement:

"I kind of have just looked at this always as, I know

the Lord made me, and I don't know exactly every-thing. You know, I believed he picked up the dust and made Adam. but really the Bible also says that the day is as a thousand years, and a thousand years is a day."

So long as one affirms that "God did it," it apparently would not disturb this student if one affirmed that the divine method was an evolutionary process over vast ages of time. To her, the entire matter is rather irrelevant if one will but acknowledge that God was involved in the process. Hear her again:

"I don't see the good in the argument—if some will say that God made us—there's so much more to our lives right now. We are here now, and I just have never been offended [by these professors' explana-tions of origins] and I can't think of any other stu-dent that has."

She then went on to point out that the "day/age" concept was the way by which Manis explained the creation "days" of Genesis 1.

Finally, there is something about this Petition that is highly suspicious. First, the author says that "some are trying to have Dr. Archie Manis and Dr. Ken Williams removed from their positions as professors at ACU." Second, however, she confidently declares that "the administration is supporting our teachers." Third, she urges students to sign the Petition and/or write a letter to no less an official than Dr. C.G. Gray, Vice-President of Academic Affairs (why assume his involve-ment, for example, and not the department head?). She even knows that either mailing the forms or dropping them by Dr. Gray's office will be acceptable. Does it not seem uncommonly strange that a mere biology student has this much insight into such a sensitive matter which the University had been (for many months) desperately trying to conceal?? We have talked with other students on the ACU campus who, up to this point, had not heard one whisper about this scandal. It appears highly likely to this writer that this impressionable young woman was "used" as a pawn in this ugly cover-up that ACU officials were attempting to perpetrate. This Student Petition is, therefore, just one more piece of incriminating evidence in this scandalous episode.

The Myth About The Manis "Myth" and the December 8, 1985 Manis Public Statement

One of the most colossal blunders made in this entire matter was when Archie Manis decided to write, in his own script, the term "myth" in the margin of Genesis 1. What a thorn in his side that notation has been. What an embarrassment it has been to ACU administrators as they have sought to defend the professor. Please take another look at the photo-reproduction of that reference (p 16); it is important that this image be sharp in your mind as we discuss certain factors relating to it.

Observe that Dr. Manis has characterized Genesis 1:1-2:3 as "Creation Hymn, Myth #1".

First, why has the narrative been dubbed a "hymn"? Religious modernists have applied a variety of appellations to Genesis 1 and 2 in order to negate the view that this narrative is a plain, literal, historical document which, of course, they cannot endorse while subscribing to the evolutionary concept. It has been called "legend," "myth," "saga," "hymn," "poetry," "drama," "parable," etc. It is none of these. Chapters 1 and 2 are written in the same general style as the balance of the Genesis record; the characteristics of poetry or hymnology are totally lacking. (Compare, for example, Psalm 104:5-9—a clear example of the creation events with a poetic motif.) The use of the term "hymn" as a descriptive of Genesis 1 reveals more about Manis than he intended.

Dr. Manis' use of the terms "hymn" and "myth" has created such a storm of controversy that, in order to save face, he has been forced to create his own definitions of those terms. For instance, in a defense he made of his writings before the Baker Heights church in Abilene, on December 8, 1985, Manis claimed, with reference to the term "hymn,"—"The word 'hymn' denotes quite appropriately the brevity, grace, and beauty of the Genesis account, and it never pretended to say anything else." A man who uses words in such an unconventional fashion does not need to be teaching school; he needs to go back to school! The truth is, his new-found definitions are a "patch-up" job to save his faculty status at ACU!

Second, there is the word "myth." The use of the term "myth" with reference to the Genesis account is certainly no surprise to anyone familiar with the literature of religious liberalism. That word abounds in the modernists' vocabulary. For example, note the following:

> "Obviously the book [Genesis] **begins in that misty region of tradition and transmitted myth in which imagination precedes knowledge.** . . .So all imaginative stories, including the element of myth, which form part of the early chapters of the Bible are the efforts of men to put truth into pictures" (*The Interpreter's Bible*, Abingdon, New York, 1952, Vol. I, pp 460, 463, emphasis added).

So, we are perfectly acquainted with how "myth" is employed in connection with Genesis 1-2, and no fanciful, desperate rationalization of Manis is going to conceal this fact. And yet this is precisely how the professor has attempted to deal with this exposure. In his December 8 statement to the Baker Heights church, Manis, in attempting to justify his use of "myth," declared:

> "'Myth' can be defined as a body of information essential to the understanding of a culture, whether the information is true or false. That is the way the term was used in this case."

Where on earth did Manis find such a definition for "myth"? It certainly is not in any of the standard language authorities we have consulted. We suggest the "definition" is solely that of Manis himself—as an after-thought, in order to salvage his career.

In response to this pathetic explanation we must point out: (1) There is nothing in connection with Manis' marginal note which would suggest that he was using the term in any exceptional way. The format is identical with the other hand-writing notations on this page. (2) The most obvious impression would have to be that by the use of "myth" Manis was suggesting that Genesis was "a traditional story of unkown authorship, professing a historical basis, but serving usually to explain some phenomenon of nature, the origin of man. . . any fictitious story. . ." (Webster). The word "myth," as used in the New Testament (5 times), denotes that which stands in contrast to truth (Cf.: II Timothy 4:4). (3) Dr. Manis' explanation of his use of "myth" is not consistent with the defense made for him by Dr. C.G. Gray. In the meeting of September 13th, Gray contended that Manis employed the word "myth" in its **ordinary** meaning, (i.e., a fictional account), but that he was simply suggesting **that this was the concept argued by evolutionists.** Manis, on the other hand, now contends that he was using the term in a very legitimate fashion which was not designed to reflect upon the historicity of the Genesis record. **These two stories are galaxies apart!** The gentlemen are in such a state of panic that they can't even get their stories together. It is our considered judgment that brethren will be able to see through this semantic camouflage.

Third, religious modernists have long denied the Mosaic authorship of, and the unity between, Genesis 1 and Genesis 2. Here is a sample of the "higher critical" approach to these chapters.

> "Chapters 1-2 contain two accounts of the creation of the world by God. According to the first (1:1-2:4a), man was created, male and female (1:26, 27), after the creation of plants (1:11-12) and animals (1:20-25); according to the second (2:4b-25), man was created first (2:7), then the trees (2:9), then the animals (2:19), and finally woman (2:21-22). In view of these discrepancies, to say nothing of differences of style and feeling so obvious as to need no detailed enumeration here, the two stories cannot come from the same hand" (*The Interpreter's Bible*, I, 465).

The notation of Dr. Manis to "Creation Hymn, Myth #1 1:1-

2:3" is a clear accommodation to the Documentary Hypothesis. Here, for example, is a quotation from Dr. Manis' "Research In Genesis," a class handout.

> "(5) Describe the sequence of creation events recorded in Genesis 1, day by day; list the items and the 'creation day' for each one.
> "(6) Describe the sequence of creation events recorded in Genesis 2:4-25, day by day; list the items and the 'creation day' given for each one. [Note: Observe how "creation day" is set apart in quotation marks. BT]
> "(7) Discuss the differences between the two 'creation hymns' (5 and 6 above). Are these two accounts of the same creation story, or is this repetition with a change in sequence?"

Does this sound familiar? Compare it with the quotation from *The Interpreter's Bible* cited above.

In passing we simply cannot resist calling attention to the fact that Christ did not consider Genesis 1 and 2 as two "creation hymns." He quoted from both chapters 1 and 2 **in the same sentence**, even joining them by the conjunction "and" without giving the slightest hint that He was dealing with two separate narratives (Cf.: Matthew 19:4, 5). Moreover, liberal writers generally ignore the fact that in Genesis 2, Moses simply focuses more sharply upon the origin of man. The sequence there is not intended to be chronological, as in Genesis 1. Conservative scholars have dealt with this fact for centuries and it is inexcusable that one who is directing "research in Genesis" should appear to be unaware of it.

Since we are briefly discussing Dr. Manis' "Research in Genesis," there is one additional matter that we would highlight. After making various assignments regarding the text of Genesis 1 and 2, the professor instructed his students:

> "You also need to present a carefully written, documented or annotated statement of the **modern, synthetic view of evolution**. Include a discussion of plate tectonics, sea floor spreading, and continental drift.

Finally, synthesize these two studies into a personal statement of belief about origins" [Emphasis BT].

There it is in living color! Combine your views about Genesis with the modern concept of evolution, and formulate your personal belief about origins. One would be hard pressed to find a better statement of **THEISTIC EVOLUTION!** Can there be any question in the minds of reasonable people as to what has been transpiring at Abilene Christian University?

Evolution, Purpose, and Values

One of the most incredible statements that this writer has ever read from one who professes to be a Christian educator is contained in Archie Manis' "Evolution Notes" (p 4). Hear him.

> "Meaning and purpose in human life are found among theists, atheists, and agnostics. It is the burden and the responsibility of all human beings to seek those values, whether from the tenets of a specific religion or from the experience and wisdom of our past and present cultures. Neo-Darwinism will neither destroy not [sic] provide the need for values, but it does force us to expand our views of life, time, and the human condition."

There are several observations that we would make regarding this unbelievable statement.

(1) **Atheism's Purpose In Life**—Atheists have long struggled with the problem of finding "purpose in life" if man is a mere cosmic accident. Time and again they have conceded that there simply is no purpose in the evolutionary process. Listen to Dr. George Simpson:

> "It [evolution] turns out to be basically materialistic, with no sign of purpose as a working variable in life history. . . . Discovery that the universe apart from man or before his coming lacks and lacked any purpose or plan has the inevitable corollary that the

workings of the universe cannot provide any auto-
matic, universal, eternal, or absolute ethical criteria
of right and wrong. This discovery has completely
undermined all older attempts to find an intuitive
ethic or to accept such an ethic as revelation" (*The
Meaning of Evolution*, Yale University Press, New
Haven, Connecticut, 3rd Printing, 1961, pp 230,
345).

To suggest, therefore, that an atheist can find "meaning and
purpose" in life is to utter an absurdity.

(2) **Values For Life**—Next, Manis contends that human
beings have the responsibility to seek "values" for living. Well,
precisely **where** shall those values be sought? Does this Christian teacher (and elder in the church) recommend the biblical
revelation as the source of man's ethical and moral values?
Not even remotely! Those values may be sought "from the
tenets of a specific religion [will just any religion do?] or from
the experience and wisdom of our past and present cultures."
Does man "hammer out" his own value system upon the basis
of experience and human wisdom? I tell you, this is absolutely
amazing.

Finally, Manis informs his students that Neo-Darwinism
is not dangerous at all. It neither provides nor destroys the
need for values. It simply expands our consciousness of life,
time, and the human condition. Here is an interesting question.
If Manis does not believe that man is the result of an evolutionary process [God's method of bringing humanity to its
present status], what is the meaning of his statement that Neo-
Darwinism forces us to "expand our views" of the "human
condition"? What else would the man have to say to convince
you that he is, in fact, a **THEISTIC EVOLUTIONIST?**

Further, consider these additional admissions which Dr.
Manis made in his public statement on December 8 to the
Baker Heights congregation. In discussing his "Research in
Genesis" handouts (the ones in which he labelled Genesis 1
and 2 as "myth"), Dr. Manis stated: "It was given with a text
of the RSV of Genesis 1 and 2 that had hand notations I had
made in the margins. It was used as an illustration of an assignment I had made in a zoology class. It was not an assignment

for seminar." I must candidly admit that I am constantly amazed at Dr. Manis' inability to get his facts, and his story, straight! It seems that every time he attempts to "explain" something, he only succeeds in making matters worse. For example, notice two very important points here. First, he openly and freely admits that **these same handouts have been used previously** in his other classes! So now we have the situation where not only biology seminar students, but also zoology students have been exposed to these materials as well! Second, notice that Dr. Manis clearly states that "Research in Genesis" was an assignment he had made for "a zoology class" and that "It was not an assignment for seminar." Now, return to page 13 in this book, examine Dr. Manis' "Evolution Notes," (which **were** used in the seminar class!) and scrutinize his point #18 which specifically states: "Refer to the 'Research in Genesis' handout." Viola! How can Dr. Manis honestly expect us to believe that he passed out to his seminar students his "Evolution Notes" that direct the student to refer to "Research in Genesis" and yet he never meant "Research in Genesis" for his seminar students' use? Both stories cannot be true! On the one hand he tells the students to specifically refer to "Research in Genesis" (#18, "Evolution Notes") and on the other hand he tries to get us to believe that he never even intended "Research in Genesis" for his seminar students' use (December 8 statement to Baker Heights congregation)!? We cannot help but wonder, which are we supposed to believe— his **written directions to the students BEFORE** all of this controversy, or his attempted "explanation" **AFTER** his errors were discovered?

In addition to these statements made publicly on December 8, Dr. Manis also stated the following: "It may help you to know that my seminar was a one-time, specialty class, as seminars usually are. Neither the subject nor the textbook are part of a regular curriculum for biology majors,..." Why would Dr. Manis make such statements, when he full well knows they are false?! **He** was the teacher for a biology seminar class in the spring of 1984 (remember Brenda Lobley?) when the topic for the entire seminar class was once again **evolution** (unrefuted!). How can Dr. Manis state that this was a "one-time, specialty class"? It most certainly was not! In fact, if you will notice, his "Research in Genesis" handouts are even **dated** "March 15, 1983"! So much for that argument!

The "Accuracy" of the "Intensive Investigation" by the ACU Board—The December 10 Letter Authored by Board Member, Dub Orr

It is indeed difficult to identify **just** one or two events out of this entire sordid series, which began almost one year ago, that represent(s) the most significant blunders on the part of the ACU faculty and administration, because there have been several. One of course, as we have already stated, was Dr. Archie Manis' labelling of Genesis 1 and 2 as "myth." Another, in this writer's estimation, is the **continued** inability of the ACU people involved to "get their stories" straight. The conflicting, and contradictory, "explanations" of these events of the past eleven or twelve months continue to issue forth from those associated with ACU in one capacity or another, and get more ludicrous with each passing day. For example, the University has repeatedly changed its stance on the teaching of evolution by its professors. First, University officials flatly denied that evolution was being taught. Second, in a complete about-face, in the September 13 meeting University officials stated that yes, evolution **was** taught, but only in such a classroom dialogue as to be refuted. Third, then one of the professors involved, Dr. Archie Manis, stated (in front of several witnesses on **two different occasions**) that he taught evolution in his classes **without refutation.** Now, apparently the University has made yet another about-face in stating that it **is** teaching evolution, but only in order to prepare its students for higher education purposes (Cf.: Dr. C.G. Gray's admissions in the *Abilene Reporter-News*, Monday, December 16, p 1). One is made to wonder **which** of these conflicting stories (if any?!) is the **correct** response from the University!

Even sadder is this: apparently the inability of some at ACU to deal in a straightforward way with plain, simple facts is like a disease which is rapidly spreading. Not only are professors and on-campus administrators afflicted by it, but now it is clear that even Board Members are involved. As proof of that statement, we offer the following. On December 2, 1985

Mr. & Mrs. Jerry Lobley of Texline, Texas wrote a letter to Dr. Bill Teague to complain about the teaching of evolution, as factual and without refutation, to their daughter Brenda. They had made it clear, in a previous letter to Dr. Teague, that as a result of this teaching at ACU, Brenda was now experiencing faith problems. Did they get a response from Dr. Teague? They did not! Did he write them any kind of personal letter? He did not! And so, on December 2, Mrs. Lobley wrote to say how disappointed she was that he would not even honor them with a personal response to what they deemed so serious a matter—their child's soul.

On December 10, one of the members of the Board of Trustees, Dub Orr, wrote Mrs. Lobley a letter in response to her letter to Dr. Teague (notice: **still** no personal response from the President!!!). Mr. Orr, you will remember, was the Board member who was present in **both** the September 13 and November 17 meetings which I had with University officials. And you will remember from reading previous sections of this book that it was Mr. Orr who was telephoned by Dale Burleson of Oskaloosa, Iowa so that he (Dale) could inform Mr. Orr of how, as early as 1972, Dr. Kenneth Williams had taught evolution **without refutation.** And, this is the same Mr. Orr who, along with another Board member, personally interviewed Mark Scott for approximately two hours on these very matters. With these things fresh on your mind, listen to the statements made to Mrs. Lobley by Mr. Orr. In spite of the fact that both **present and former** students had already affirmed to him that evolution was being, and had been, taught as factual, Mr. Orr wrote to the Lobleys as follows: "It may be at this point that I have lost all credibility with you and Jerry, but I would like for you to know that I believe with all my heart that there is no present advocacy of organic evolution in the Biology department at ACU" (Orr letter, p 2). Mr. Orr had more to say, however, which will be of interest to honest readers. He stated: "I can only certify that after over forty hours of personal investigation and involvement, the truth is that organic evolution is not being advocated in ACU classes" (p 4). But, prior to that concluding statement, he said: "As I told you in our telephone conversation, **there has been careless handling of the subject of organic evolution in the past**—in the area of handouts which were not disclaimed in writing or on the handout, and also in the area of not actively refuting organic evolution. The offending hand-outs were used in only one seminar, which has never been taught before the spring of 1985 by Dr. Manis and will not be taught in the future by him. The hand-outs represent a one-time error, and they will never be re-used" (p 3, emphasis added).

The following points **must** be made regarding these statements. After reading them, any honest inquirer will quickly see what we mean when we say that the folks at ACU are having loads of trouble "getting their stories straight." Also, the facts that you are about to read will show you the "accuracy" of this "intense" investigation at ACU. Observe the following.

(1) Mr. Orr plainly **admits** that there has been "careless handling of the subject of organic evolution" on the ACU campus. In what way? Oh, handouts have been used which taught evolution as factual, but which were not disclaimed. And? **Evolution has not been actively refuted!** May I kindly ask this question: What would one have to do to **teach** evolution besides handing out materials presenting it as fact (without any disclaimer), and then **not refuting it**? Does brother Orr think that we are so "dense" that we cannot understand what he has just said? Well, we are not!

(2) Now, notice Mr. Orr's next statement: "The offending hand-outs were used in only one seminar, which has never been taught before the spring of 1985 by Dr. Manis. . ." Can you believe that? In the September 13 meeting I plainly told Mr. Orr (and the other ACU people present) that Brenda Lobley took seminar class **under Dr. Manis** in the spring of 1984! And, in a telephone conversation with the Lobleys (the same one to which his letter alludes) the Lobleys themselves told Mr. Orr that it was in a 1984 **seminar class under Dr. Manis** in which Brenda was taught evolution as fact. Mr. Orr says that never before the spring of 1985 has Dr. Manis taught seminar class. How in the world can he say such a thing, when he knows it to be patently false?! To the reader we say this: Take a quick look at the **date** on Dr. Manis' "Research in Genesis" handouts which are reproduced elsewhere in this book. You will notice that they are dated by him, "15 March, 1983"! And, true to what the Lobleys and their daughter have said,

Brenda Lobley took seminar class under Dr. Manis that very next year—in the spring of 1984! How, then, can Mr. Orr state so blatantly (when he has been told just the opposite on at least three different occasions) that Dr. Manis has "never before" taught seminar? We would like an answer to that!

(3) But, that is just the hem of the proverbial garment. Notice this: Mr. Orr stated that the handouts were used in "only one seminar" class. Oh? That is **not what Dr. Manis himself has publicly stated!** In Manis' December 8 statement before the Baker Heights congregation, he plainly admitted (listen carefully): "The other handout being quoted as evidence against me is titled 'Research in Genesis.' It was given with a text of the RSV of Genesis 1 and 2 that had hand notions I had made in the margins [labelling Genesis 1 & 2 as "myth"—BT]. **It was used as an illustration of an assignment I had made in zoology class**" (Manis statement, p 1). So, Mr. Orr's statement is proven false by the very man he has been attempting to protect throughout this whole ordeal. Now which statement (and which man) are we to believe? Mr. Orr attempts to get the Lobleys to believe that the handouts are a "one-time" occurrence, used only a single time in a single seminar class. Dr. Manis, on the other hand, admits that he has used these very handouts in **seminar classes AND in zoology classes.** Obviously both men's statements cannot be true. Why is it that these folks from ACU can't get their stories together? "Oh the tangled web we weave, when first we practice to deceive."

(4) We would be quite remiss if we did not call attention to one other statement from Mr. Orr. Perhaps he thought it would go unnoticed. It has **not**! He commented that, "The hand-outs represent a one-time error, and they will never be re-used." First, of course, we now know that the handouts had been used **repeatedly**, not just once. But examine the statement more closely. "The hand-outs represent a one-time **ERROR**..." A what? **AN ERROR**!! But wait. The people from ACU have repeatedly tried to convince us, and others, that the hand-outs have been "quoted out of context." In fact, Dr. Teague made that very statement to the *Abilene Reporter-News* interviewer, and was quoted as such in the Monday, December 16 article. If we have quoted the handouts "out of context," why then

is one of the ACU Board members (who has, by the way, **seen** the handouts) calling them an **ERROR**? Think about this important point for just a moment. If the handouts **are** being used "out of context" by us (and we deny that they are), how could they then be used by the very professors themselves "in the proper context" and **still** be called by the ACU Board member an "ERROR"?? What is it about the handouts that would be **erroneous**? Mr. Orr will most certainly not tell you what it is he thinks is "in error" about the handouts, because he is caught up in a desperate defense of the two professors. So, allow **us** to tell you what is "in error" about the handouts. They called evolution a **fact**, and taught that Genesis 1 and 2 are a "myth." **That's what is "in error" about the handouts!** Why, oh why, cannot these folks from ACU see that? And why can they not see how much damage they are doing to their own cause by producing so much varied, conflicting, and contradictory testimony in their cover-up?

By way of summary in this section, let us remind the reader of the facts herein discussed:

(A) Dub Orr, an ACU Board member, specifically states that there has been "careless handling of organic evolution" on the ACU campus.

(B) Mr. Orr confesses that evolution has **not been actively refuted**.

(C) Mr. Orr admits that handouts which are "in error" have been used, **without any disclaimer**.

(D) Mr. Orr states that Dr. Archie Manis had never before the spring of 1985 taught a biology seminar class, when in reality, he **has** taught at least one other such class that can be (and has been) documented!

(E) Mr. Orr contends that these "erroneous" handouts have not been used elsewhere, but are a "one-time error." In fact, the handouts **had** been used in 1983, 1984, and 1985— and who knows when else?!

(F) University officials continue to maintain that **we** have "quoted out of context" the handouts. Mr. Orr states that the handouts are "in error"—so much so that they will not be used again. [QUESTION: If this whole issue regarding the handouts **is** "our fault" and the handouts have simply been "quoted out of context," **WHY** is it that the handouts will never be used again?]

Now we return to our two major points of this section: the contradictory statements which continue to issue forth from those at ACU involved in this controversy, and the "accuracy" of this "intensive" investigation on the part of the ACU Board. Regarding the first point—contradictory statements—what else can we say but what has already been noted in this very section? One party says one thing; another says something else; and a third says something different. Just who are we to believe? Truth is **not contradictory**!

Regarding the second point—the accuracy of the ACU Board's "intensive" investigation—let us say this. Mr. Orr says Dr. Manis never taught seminar before. He was wrong. Mr. Orr says that handouts were used in only one class. He was wrong. Mr. Orr has stated that the handouts are being quoted "out of context." Then he himself admits they are "in error" and will "never be used again." Interpretation: he was wrong (about them being quoted out of context). Then Mr. Orr expects us to believe him when he says, "I can only certify that after forty hours of investigation and involvement, the truth is that organic evolution is not being advocated in ACU classes."

You can believe him if you so desire. But with "facts" so in error as the ones in Mr. Orr's letter, with admissions of guilt as strong as the ones he has inadvertently made, and with a story which is as self-contradictory as his, pardon us if we are a bit skeptical! Actually, this whole thing would be humorous, were it not so deadly serious!

ACU "Tips Its Hand" and Goes Public: The Editorial in the Student Newspaper, *The Optimist*

The astute reader will remember a statement made in the midst of this controversy, and quoted some few pages back, by Dr. C.G. Gray of ACU. In speaking with the elders of the 5th and Grape congregation in Abilene regarding this matter, Dr. Gray had insisted that the University was "attempting to keep this thing quiet." **NOT ANY MORE!**

On Friday, December 13, the student newspaper, *The Optimist*, ran a lengthy editorial entitled simply, "Evolution." Apparently the University has been, and is being, deluged with so many inquiries (letters, phone calls, visits, etc.) regarding this problem that upper-eschalon administrators ultimately decided that the best defense might well be a good offense. And so, in what was obviously an attempt to innoculate the students **before** they left for the Christmas holidays, the University decided to use the pages of the student newspaper, *The Optimist*, to "quell the rumors" about the teaching of evolution on the ACU campus. Timing, of course, was of the essence. The whole event was well-planned and executed. The December 13 issue of *The Optimist* was the last issue of the paper for the semester, which prevented any "Letters to the Editor" from appearing during the fall semester. And, on that same day, Dr. Teague, President of ACU, made a short speech from the platform in chapel, in which he stated that the students would possibly hear "rumors" of "charges" against the University—"rumors" and "charges" which (he assured them) were completely false. This double-barreled attack was apparently calculated to be the *coup de grace* as far as the University was concerned. The plan was to prepare the students **before** they left for home so that they could explain to their parents that "rumors" were circulating about ACU, and so dispell them. The University hoped to "get in the last word," so to speak, as the semester ended in order that no rebuttal from any source would be possible.

And, it might just have worked! But the University overlooked one important point: **now** their defense was "in the open" as part of the public domain. And that meant two things: (1) those who had not previously heard about the current controversy were now hearing about it, and; (2) the "defense" could be answered—which it will be, in the very pages of the book you are now reading. It is to that "defense" that we now turn our attention.

The unsigned *Optimist* editorial was, as one might expect in a newspaper regulated and funded by the ACU administration, totally biased in favor of both ACU and the two professors involved. This, we might add, does not surprise us. Nor does it surprise us that "we" are termed the "accuser" and made to be the "bad guy" in this whole ordeal. From the very beginning of this controversy, almost one year ago, we have known that there was a strong possibility that pursuing these matters would cause us to be labeled, and to possibly even lose friends. However, we have long believed that a faithful Christian does **not** count the consequences **first** and **then** stand for the Truth; rather, the faithful child of God stands for the Truth **regardless** of the consequences. From that belief we will not waiver. And so, though we have been made, at least by this particular campus paper editorial, to appear as the "troubler of Israel," we firmly believe that once the facts of the case are heard, Truth will be vindicated in the hearts of honest men and women.

As the *Optimist* editorial began, the tone was set for what was to follow. The first sentences of the article stated: "The university needs the brotherhood to express a genuine and undying interest in the welfare of Christian education. However, the university is being damaged by a few Christians who, claiming interest, have recently disrupted the campus and the brotherhood with rumors and unjustified accusations. These accusers have the biology department in their sights; they charge Drs. Archie Manis and Ken Williams with teaching evolution as fact. This charge is unjustified. The university supports these two biology professors and is taking a firm position in refuting the charges."

These statements, which are obviously intended to "tug at the heartstrings" of the ACU community, contain a mixture of truth and error. It is true: the university **does** need the brotherhood to express a genuine interest in Christian education. [Parenthetically, we might add that it is refreshing to see that at least **someone** on the campus of ACU feels that brotherhood support **is** required. Up to now, exactly the opposite has been the attitude expressed. We have been told that ACU does not have to aquiesce to "outside pressures" from those in the brotherhood, and that the University will jolly well do as it pleases. I must admit to being a bit surprised to see, then, this statement as the very first words of the article!] And, it is true that we have charged Drs. Archie Manis and Ken Williams with teaching evolution as fact. In addition, it is most certainly a true statement that "the university supports these two biology professors."

However, the first four paragraphs of the *Optimist* article, which we have quoted above, also contain points that are seriously in error. For example, the charge is made that disruption has occurred on campus because of "rumors and unjustified accusations." Oh?! Lest the reader accept that statement as true—that the charges made were nothing more than "rumors" or were "unjustified"—we suggest that you return to the previous pages of this book and re-read the summary assessment (as signed by the neutral witness who was present, James D. Willeford, elder, 5th and Grape Street congregation in Abilene), of the September 13 meeting which I had with ACU administrators. After reading that summary and observing the complete inability of anyone present representing ACU to either discount or adequately answer those statements— does it sound to you like we are here dealing with just "rumors" or "unjustified" accusations? When the Dean of the College of Biblical Studies states that the materials produced by the professors are "rotten" and "pathetic" (to use his own words), does that then somehow magically transform the charges into "rumors" that are "unjustified"? We think not!

The *Optimist* article also states that we "have the biology department" in our sights. Not true! As I stated in the Preface to this volume, our accusations have **never** been against an **entire department**, or even the ACU community as a whole. I have long loved, and respected, such biology professors as Dr. Clark Stevens, Dr. F.M. Churchill, Mr. Roy Shake, and others. And so it is totally incorrect to state that we have the "biology department" (as a whole) "in our sights." Further, the editor/author seems to feel that we are merely "claiming interest"—the intent of that statement being to cast doubt upon our motives in this investigation. Once again, we have stated our intent in the Preface to this volume. We do not just "claim" interest. We **have** a **genuine interest** in what is taught, and how it is taught, on the campus of ACU, because we have for many years loved and respected this institution. May it be so again!

The remainder of the *Optimist* article is of much the same genre. Some truth; much error. It would be literally impossible, in the space allotted in this small book, to deal in an indepth fashion with each erroneous point made by the author of the article. However, lest some should think that the errors cannot be answered, we will take valuable space to briefly respond to what we believe to be serious breaches of the truth regarding these matters.

First, the article points out that "Manis and Williams profess a strong belief in the Genesis account of creation." So does every theistic evolutionist, mitigated evolutionist, and progressive creationist with which we have ever dealt! As brother Swift so aptly pointed out in his 33-page document dealing with Archie Manis' errors, that is one reason why these men have been able to move so effectively among us for so long—because folks would ask them: "Do you believe in the Genesis account of creation?" and they would answer, "Of course!" But that is the wrong question. The question is not **just** whether or not they "profess a strong belief" in the Genesis account of creation. The **real** questions (which we are seemingly unable to get the University or the professors to answer) are these: (A) What do you believe about organic and/or theistic evolution? (B) Do you refute organic and/or theistic evolution? (C) Do you accept Genesis as literal and historical, complete with a six-literal-day creation? (D) Do you oppose the idea that Genesis is mythical and/or allegorical? It may do for the professors to look at an 18 or 19-year old student and say, "I believe in the Genesis account of creation." But it will **not** do for them to look at some of us who have spent our entire adult lives in the midst of the creation/evolution controversy, and who have debated both atheistic and theistic evolutionists over these very points, and make the same statement. We are not that easily fooled. And that, of course, brings up the question that has been asked many times throughout this entire ordeal, and throughout this entire book: **WHY** could the professors not prepare, and sign, the statement requested of them in the September 13 meeting? You be the judge! I already know.

The article goes on to say that "the accusers have shown an incredible persistence, despite the fact that the professors, the students in the professors' classes, the department head, the dean of the college, the Board of Trustees and the university as a whole have refuted the charges and attempted to quell these debilitating accusations." Once again the editor/author presents a mixture of truth and error, in an attempt to make all the statements look like truth. For example, it is true that I have shown "incredible persistence." In fact, that point should be the least shocking (to ACU administrators) of any other single thing in this entire controversy. Why? Because I told them in my earliest letters that this matter would not "go away" just because they chose to ignore it. I specifically alerted them to the fact that I would, indeed, be "persistent." I have kept my word—apparently to their surprise and chagrin.

But the remainder of the statement we have just quoted is false. How can the editor/author make the statement that "...the professors, the students in the professors' classes, the department head, the dean of the college, the Board of Trustees and the university as a whole have refuted the charges" when the only items I have received from the University throughout this entire ordeal have been (1) a three-paragraph note from Dean Perry Reeves asking me to pray for the University as it seeks to fulfill its mission, and; (2) statements from the professors (finally!) stating that they believe in God, the Bible, Christ, and creation?? I have met, personally, with ACU officials in two separate meetings, and in neither of them was any explanation forthcoming to the charges that I have made. They stated that they were "working" on the problem (at least that is what I was told during the second, November 17 meeting). And when I asked for specific things that had been, or were being done, to "correct" the problem, the only answer I received (from Board Member Dub Orr) was that he "thought" the professors had been "spoken to about these things." Oh, well, that makes everything alright!? Why are we being told that these folks at ACU have "refuted" the charges, when in fact, just the opposite is true? They have continually attempted a massive cover-up, as is evidenced by the fact that they refused (upon orders directly from the Board of Trustees) to respond to my letters. They promised to have the two professors sign documents, the contents of which were agreed upon in the September 13 meeting, but failed to keep their word. They have changed their story on whether or not (or why?) they are teaching evolution—and changed it at least three times! They have admitted to using handouts in the professors classes that are "in error" (see Dub Orr's December 10 letter to the Lobleys). They have admitted that "our aprons are not exactly clean" (see the Willeford document, where Dub Orr is quoted) in regard to teaching evolution without any refutation whatsoever. They have admitted that "there has been careless handling of the subject of organic evolution in the past" (see Dub Orr's December 10 letter to the Lobleys). And now, suddenly, the *Optimist* article arrives, and "everything" has been "refuted." This must be the stuff of which fairy tales are made, for it most surely is not reality!

The *Optimist* article also states: "We think the most incomprehensible factor in this situation is the fact that it only took one dissatisfied student to cause so much hurt and pain." Here we go again. It's the old addage that "if you say something long enough, and often enough, folks will eventually begin to believe it." I think there are actually **some** on the ACU campus who **really believe** that there was just one miserable, maladjusted, malevolent student who caused all of this. Nothing could be farther from the truth! And, anyone who has read this far in this book has surely figured that out for themselves by now. What about Brenda Lobley's testimony? Does it count for nothing? And what about the testimony of Kent West? Does it count for nothing? And what about Dale Burleson's testimony? Does it, too, count for nothing? And, there are others who have asked that their names not be used, because they fear that the same thing(s) that happened to Mark Scott (what about Mark's testimony—does it count for nothing?) will happen to them? You see, it is so easy for the author of the *Optimist* article to make one poor, misguided soul the "cause" of this whole thing. In reality, as ironic as it may seem to some, it is actually ACU who is responsible for all that has happened. Had they answered our letters, and been willing to work with us to a satisfactory conclusion from the very beginning, none of this would be happening. Instead, they chose to ignore plain, simple inquiries into their teachings (I can understand why now!), and they chose to cover-up gross violations of their original charter as well as multitudes of false teachings that have been propagated since at least 1972!! Yet we are now told it is the "fault" of one "dissatisfied student." Oh, how they wish! For, then it would be so much easier for them to whitewash the whole sordid affair.

But the whitewash—the attempted cover-up—will not succeed. For now it is no longer "just one dissatisfied student" who has stepped forward to expose the error of Manis and

Williams. Consider this if you will. On December 11, 1985, Dr. Furman Kearley, currently Editor of the *Gospel Advocate*, and formerly Director of Graduate Bible Studies at Abilene Christian University, penned a six-page, single-spaced letter to Dub Orr, the member of the Board of Trustees who has been so involved in this sad series of events. Furman forwarded to us a copy of his letter to Mr. Orr. Upon receiving it, we telephoned Furman, and were told that Dub had requested that Furman "give his input" into the situation at ACU. Furman's letter of December 11 was for that expressed purpose. I doubt seriously that Dub Orr would have asked for such input if he could have seen **beforehand** what Furman was about to write. With Furman's permission, a portion of his letter is reproduced below. As you read it, remember two things: (1) Furman was contacted by Dr. C.G. Gray when my first letter to Manis and Williams arrived, as Dr. Gray bemoaned the fact that I had asked his faculty members questions about their beliefs; Furman answered the questions in less than ten minutes, and suggested that the two professors do likewise! In other words, Furman has been apprised of this situation from the very beginning. He has also seen most of the evidence which is in existence regarding these matters. (2) Also remember ACU's petty lament that all of this is the result of "just one dissatisfied student" when you read Furman's documentation that these things have been going on at the ACU campus **for the past five years at least!** Furman heard Dr. Kenneth Williams, approximately five years ago, give a speech to the ACU faculty that was "peppered throughout with evolutionary and uniformitarian terminology" (to use Furman's exact words). Moreover, Furman mentioned in his letter that he himself had heard "complaints from various students from time to time" about the treatment of evolution in the ACU biology department. And, as you read the following paragraphs from Furman's letter, notice his conclusions regarding the professors' statements, their refusal to answer our questions, and the use of the words "hymn" and "myth" in their presentations. And remember as you read that these statements are from a man who was a co-faculty member with Williams and Manis, and who served as the Director of Graduate Bible Studies at ACU! (Now what was that about "just one dissatisfied student?")

_____

"Dear Dub:

". . .Personally, I heard Brother Ken Williams give a speech to the faculty some five years ago or so. His speech was peppered throughout with evolutionary and uniformitarian terminology. I marked down then in my mind that he accepted and believed far more of the theory of evolution than was healthy. I shared my concern with two or three of the administrators, but so far as I know, nothing was ever pursued concerning the matter. That's all I know firsthand. . . .

"The most serious charge I would make is that the longer it goes that the men charged refuse to make a clear statement as to what they believe about the Bible and evolution, the more it appears that they believe something about evolution and the Bible that they do not want the brotherhood to know. When Brother Gray called this problem to my attention last spring, I filled out the questionnaire in less than 10 minutes. I returned it to him and said that all the men would have to do to stop the charges would be to fill out the questionnaire and return it. While I had a few problems with some of the "yes" and "no" questions, I made explanatory comments on only about three or four of them. If one does not believe in evolution, he would not have any problem in filling out that questionnaire and perhaps making a few explanatory comments.

"Brother Gray seemed to discard the idea of the filling out of the questionnaire, and then I suggested that they write in their own words a clear statement of their beliefs. More than eight months have passed and they still have not made a clear statement of their beliefs. I for one cannot have confidence in them any longer until they do make clear their stand on Genesis 1-11 and the relation of the theory of evolution to it. The statement that Brother Manis made is far too inadequate. There are hundreds of professors who have wiggled their way into universities by saying that they believe the Bible, but who really meant by that, that they believe some kind of inspiration like Shakespearean inspiration, and they had no problem with the Bible containing myth and legend. Theological school faculties are full of professors who are theistic evolutionists, who believe the Bible in their broad definition, but who say that Genesis 1-11 is written in 'theological language.' Whenever one uses such terms as 'hymn,' 'theological language,' 'myth' and so forth, beware—he is simply saying that it doesn't mean what it says, that it is not literally true. . . .

Fraternally,
(signed) F. Furman Kearley"

There you have it. Now compare such comments with the editorial in the *Optimist* which stated that "so much hurt and pain" have been caused by just one "dissatisfied student." Hardly! The "hurt and pain" have been caused **not** by the student(s), but rather by the professors who teach evolution as fact, present evolution without any refutation whatsoever, and advocate Genesis 1-2 as mythical! The feeble attempt of ACU administrators to lay the burden of guilt at the feet of "just one student" will not be tolerated. Let the administrators and professors bear the guilt. It belongs on their shoulders, not on the shoulders of those who have stood faithfully for the word of God!

The *Optimist* editor/author makes yet another blunder in the article under review. The statement is made: "Throughout correspondence with various administrative channels, the accusations remained unwaivering: evolution was being taught as fact. The accuser would not accept the university's assurance that not only was this untrue, but were it true, the university would dismiss the professors from their teaching positions immediately." Let us examine these comments. The editor seems to think that I did not trust ACU officials when they "assured" me that everything was fine. How right the editor is! And the very next point the editor made explains the reason why. A word regarding this is certainly in order. The reader will perhaps remember the following incident, as recorded in the Willeford assessment of the September 13 meeting. Dub Orr asked me if I wanted the University to "fire" these two professors? My response, as recorded in brother Willeford's assessment, was that I wanted the University to keep its word. And I explained that statement. Dr. Perry Reeves, Dean of the College of Natural and Applied Sciences had, just a few days earlier, made the statement to Dr. Furman Kearley, who was at that time Director of Graduate Bible Studies at ACU, and who now is the Editor of the *Gospel Advocate*, that if evidence could be presented to him to prove that Manis and Williams **were** teaching evolution, they would be fired. I asked Dr. Reeves if he had, in fact, made such a statement. He said he had. I then asked those assembled if Dr. Manis had walked into his freshman biology class the first day of class during the summer session, and commented, "I am an elder in the church, and I believe in evolution. I am going to teach you evolution, and you are going to believe it too." Dr. Reeves admitted that the event I had just described had, in fact, occurred. I asked those present how much **more** "proof" they needed than the words from the professor's own mouth?! Moreover, additional proof was forthcoming in that very meeting. But was Dr. Reeves true to his word? Of course he was not! Manis had written in his handouts that evolution was a "scientific fact." He had plainly called Genesis 1 and 2 a "myth." He had told his students he "believed in evolution" and they "would too." Yet he still remains a professor today! So pardon me if I am not exactly "bowled over" by the University's supposed truthfulness to its claims. The editor is correct. I "would not accept the university's assurance" that all was well in Zion. And for good reason!

The editor also notes that I asked, in the September 13 meeting with ACU officials, that the two professors sign documents containing items as outlined, and agreed to by ACU officials. But the editor fails to note that these documents were never forthcoming. The editor does note that the two professors "signed self-prepared statements." Conveniently omitted, however, from the editor's article was the fact that these two "statements" did not contain anything even remotely resembling the items agreed upon in the September 13 meeting. The article makes it appear as if the statements we requested—and which ACU officials agreed to supply— **were** forthcoming, and then we, for no apparent reason, simply rejected them! Such is most definitely **not** the case. Earlier in this book, that was made abundantly clear.

Two last points need to be addressed in this regard. The

first may not be of major importance to some, but it is to this writer, and for that reason I would like to point out the following. The *Optimist* article states: "The accuser challenged the biology professors to a debate to clear up what he perceived to be the problem—creation vs. evolution. The professors declined in the best interest of the university." In fact, quite the opposite is true. I did not challenge **them** to a debate. The facts surrounding this have already been made available in earlier chapters of this very book. It was, in fact, Dr. Manis who challenged **me**, in front of witnesses, to a **debate**. I merely **accepted** his challenge. Unfortunately, he did not have the courage of his convictions and refused to debate me, once my letter of acceptance landed on his desk. He apparently felt more adept at making innocuous challenges behind closed doors, instead of defending his erroneous positions on the public debate platform. Nevertheless, I want it clearly understood that I accepted **his** debate offer. Interesting, however, isn't it—how he declined "in the best interest of the university"??

My last point is this. The editor/author states: "The accuser should not be allowed to influence the content of biology courses at ACU. The Genesis account of creation is the only account of creation advocated by the faculty on this campus." I cannot help but wonder if the editor would have made such statements **after** seeing Archie Manis' admissions—some of which were in his own handwriting—made public in the document produced by L.D. Swift? Dr. Manis made it abundantly clear, on more than one occasion, that he **never** taught creation (he left that up to the Bible department, remember?), but that he **did** teach evolution, and **without refutation**. In fact, Dub Orr, in his December 10 letter to Mr. & Mrs. Lobley, clearly stated that in the past evolution had been taught "without refutation."

How is it then, we would like to know, that the editor can summon the audacity to state that the professors "advocate only the Genesis account of creation"? Such is most certainly **not** the case, and apparently has not been for a long, long time. May it be so in the future!

ACU Makes The Headlines

On Monday, December 16th, 1985, the evening edition of the *Abilene Reporter-News* contained the following front-page headline, "Evolution rears its head at ACU." The article, containing approximately 37 column inches of space, was authored by Senior Staff Writer, Jerry Reed. The report was actually a very fair presentation, though some have complained that it was slanted against the University. We will not argue the point. However, the wording of the headline may be indicative of Mr. Reed's perception of this matter.

We really have very little to say about this article; most of the issues are thoroughly explored elsewhere in this volume and it is unnecessary to review them here. We would, however, like to briefly comment upon a few matters.

We were contacted by Mr. Reed on Friday, December 13th. He wanted an interview. My colleague, Wayne Jackson, and I had—even prior to Mr. Reed's call—already discussed our plan of action in case any news reporters should contact us in regard to this controversy. We determined that we would not discuss these matters with any secular journalist. However, in the course of our conversation with Mr. Reed, he informed us that Dr. C.G. Gray, of ACU, had already granted him an interview. We thus felt, at this point, that we had every right to issue a statement defending our course of action in the ACU evolution scandal. We must say, though, that we regret that ACU administrators, instead of cleaning up this mess at home, chose to "air their dirty laundry" before the world.

The news article quotes ACU President William Teague concerning the Manis class handouts, "Evolution Notes" and "Research in Genesis," in which the claims are made that "the fact of evolution is beyond dispute" and the Genesis record is a "hymn, myth." Teague charges that "the handouts were taken out of context." How in the world could the handouts be "out of context" when the **entire documents**, with absolutely no deletions, were offered as evidence? When an **entire** context is available, it can hardly be "out of context." This is but another example of President Teague's ineptitude in this business; he has, as a matter of fact, handled this entire matter with the finesse of that proverbial bull in a china shop!

The claim is made that the professors, after a thorough investigation, have been exonerated. That "investigation" has about as much credibility as Frank James investigating Jesse. Oddly enough, one of the investigators characterized Manis' teaching as "rotten" and "pathetic"; another charged that the professor has "diarrhea of the mouth" and that he acts "crazy." Not even we, Manis' critics, have been so harsh and crude.

The chief defense that the University is making is that the students are standing behind the teachers.

We certainly do not doubt that this is largely true—and for a number of reasons. First, our brethren, generally speaking, have done such a poor job of teaching our youth Christian evidences that most of our young people entering college would not recognize theistic evolution if they met it in the middle of the road at high noon. Bless their hearts, they are sincere, but they just don't pick up on many of these crucial matters. As long as the professors say, "God did it," there's no big deal as to the "how." Second, most students, who are struggling their way through college, simply want to get through it all as quickly as possible so as to make their way out into the real world. They want the respect and admiration of their professors—especially at grade time. They are not likely to make any waves. Too, they have pride in their University; they will usually strongly resist any suspicion of corruption. This is only natural. It does, however, put their "support" in its proper perspective. Finally, no amount of well-meaning "support" can negate cold, hard evidence. And that is what has incriminated these instructors. Manis and Williams have been "caught," and the point is absolutely beyond controversy!

Further, on Tuesday, December 17th, the *Abilene Reporter-News* published an editorial captioned, "ACU controversy—Evolution." The article suggested that a university is a "marketplace for ideas"—all kinds of ideas. The editor charged that those critical of ACU's handling of the evolution issue are somehow attempting to curtail the pursuit of true education. This writer is accused of trying "to stifle the debate, to thwart the free flow of ideas."

Nonsense! We have never argued that there should be no inclusion of evolutionary ideas in the classroom. What we have suggested is that when the evolutionists' arguments are introduced, the professors of a **Christian** university have the obligation to provide an adequate refutation of that material. In the ACU biology department, **there is no "free flow" of ideas**; only one side is given—the stagnant pool of **evolution**! And to contend that "Thompson is attempting to stifle the debate" is ludicrous. I have offered to debate both Williams and Manis, but both have refused—furthermore, the *Reporter-News* was privy to this information **before** this editorial was written. I ask you, "Is this responsible journalism?"

The *Reporter-News* article gives us strong reason to suspect that its author is a theistic evolutionist. He declares: "A number of Christian denominations, in fact, find no conflict between their beliefs and the theory of evolution, but, as we stated, we do not presume to provide answers to that dispute." The entire piece was typical of that liberalistic journalism that is so common in today's media.

We suggest that when an editorial of this "slant" commends the University for its approach to the evolution controversy, it is no compliment—not to the faculty; not to the administrators! It is but another tell-tale piece of incriminating evidence that highlights ACU's guilt in this affair.

———×××———

Summary and Conclusion

The writing of this book has been a most depressing chore. Anyone who enjoys this type of endeavor has to be a little spiritually unbalanced. But, as we observed initially, we did not choose the task. It fell into our lap. Whether this was the providence of God, we cannot for certain say. At any rate, we had two options—ignore the shocking, yet undeniable, evidence (as so many had already done in the past), or attempt to correct the situation. We chose the latter. As a consequence, we, and those who have courageously worked with us, have, at times, suffered the wrath of a corrupt power system within the church. We are now prepared to leave the final disposition of this matter to our brethren at-large, and ultimately, of course, to God Almighty Himself.

As we reflect back upon the material covered, just what has been established? How may we summarize?

First, we have demonstrated—by means of testimony, documentation, and the confession of ACU personnel, that the theory of evolution is being taught at Abilene Christian University. And this is significant, for, as you may recall, in the early phases of this controversy, it was utterly denied that evolution was being presented at ACU. Dr. Perry C. Reeves even declared that if it was revealed that anyone was teaching evolution at ACU, he was fired! So much for that joke.

Second, it has been established, from a professor's handout, that it has been taught that "the fact of evolution is beyond dispute."

Third, we have shown that Archie Manis' current explanation for this handout (namely, that it was only a collection of notes representing the evolutionists' views and not his own) is simply not the truth as evidenced by these facts: (a) When a student handed out creation materials in class, Manis commented that he wished he had the time to "refute" these arguments. (b) Manis once told his class, "There are some people outside the University community who are trying to tell me what I can and cannot teach. But they won't succeed. I'm an elder in the church, and I believe in evolution. I'm going to teach it to you, and you are going to believe it as well." (c) Manis boasted that he would like to get Thompson into a debate and "straighten him out" on the issues of evolution and creation. (d) As late as the first part of November, 1985, Manis wrote that "Our teaching at ACU has more[1] presented evolution as an explanation for the world—it has been and is being presented as a body of scientific thought **supported by a body of scientific evidence. As theory goes—there is no decisive evidence against any of these viewpoints, from science.**"

Fourth, it has been demonstrated that numerous humanistic and evolutionary oriented books and materials have been used in ACU science classes—books that are decidedly anti-biblical.

Fifth, it has been acknowledged (and this point is contested by no one) that absolutely no refutation was offered (by either Manis or Williams) to these evolutionary ideas. In other words, the students received a strong dose of evolution and anti-creationism, and **nothing but this**. All of this has been done, of course, under the guise of preparing our youth for similar assaults when they leave the protective environs of a "Christian" university. Our question is this: what could a secular graduate school or a humanistic society do more, to undermine these student's faith, than these ACU professors have already done—short of denying the actual existence of God?

Sixth, we have proven that the Genesis account has been represented as a "hymn" or a "myth."

Seventh, we have established that all of this is in direct violation of the school's original charter.

Eighth, we have shown that this detestable condition has been known, and protested, for a number of years, but it has been repeatedly ignored and concealed.

Ninth, we have revealed that students who dared to protest this vile teaching have been harrassed, intimidated, and

---

[1]See Appendix

threatened by faculty and administrators.

Tenth, we have regretably noted how this evil episode has caused hurt in the lives of a number of Christian people.

Eleventh, we have clearly established that we patiently tried to get this matter remedied in a quiet, private way, but that such proved utterly fruitless, hence, we were forced to bring it to the brotherhood's attention in order that our people might be able to subsequently make intelligent and spiritual decisions as to how they wish to continue supporting and sending students to Abilene Christian University.

This is our case. You are the jury. Judge the matter on the basis of evidence, not emotion. Then act!

APPENDIX

Since the publication of the first edition of this work, a controversy has arisen concerning one disputed word in the Archie Manis handwritten note of the "Swift Document." Our original text has one line as follows: "ACU has **more** presented evolution as an explanation for the world...." Manis has disputed this rendition, claiming that the line should read, "ACU has **never** presented evolution as an explanation for the world...." [NOTE: Manis did not contact our office about this matter; we learned of his discomfiture through one to whom he had complained.]

In response to this, we make the following observations: (a) We haven't the slightest desire to misrepresent Dr. Manis. That would not be right, and would only hurt the cause of Truth. If a mistake was made, it was an honest one. (b) Below is a photocopy of the original statement. The reader can judge for himself what it appears to say. (c) A change in that one word does not alter the fact that Manis wrote in the same paragraph [which is too large to reproduce here]: "...it [evolution] has been and is being presented as a body of scientific thought supported by a body of scientific evidence. As theory goes—there is no decisive evidence against any of these view points, from science." That is the damaging statement, and the part of the quotation which we emphasized. If Dr. Manis or any of the ACU administrators think that they can explain away this, they are free to try!

Let it be emphasized again. We would never knowingly misrepresent any element of this case. We have no need to. There is a vast amount of incriminating evidence, and no dispute over one word can change that!